TRUTH AND PREDICATION

TRUTH AND PREDICATION

DONALD DAVIDSON

The Belknap Press of
Harvard University Press
Cambridge, Massachusetts
London, England

First Harvard University Press paperback edition, 2008.

Library of Congress Cataloging-in-Publication Data

Davidson, Donald
Truth and predication / Donald Davidson.
p. cm.
Includes bibliographical references (p.) and index.
Contents: Theories of truth—What more is there to truth?—
The content of the concept of truth—The problem of predication—
Failed attempts—Truth and predication—A solution.
ISBN 978-0-674-01525-8 (cloth)
ISBN 978-0-674-03040-4 (pbk.)
1. Truth.   2. Predicate (Logic)   I. Title.

BC171.D38 2005
121—dc22   2004052904

Contents

Foreword

When my husband died, this book had already been accepted by Harvard University Press. They were waiting only for his final revisions. Marginalia and notes to himself in response to comments from the Press's outside readers indicated what some of these revisions might have been. Where his intentions were perfectly clear I have altered the text accordingly; where they were not, I have included the notes or marginalia in bracketed footnotes. There are of course other changes he would undoubtedly have wanted to make, had he been given the time.

I am deeply grateful to Brandom Fitelson, Ernie LePore, Kirk Ludwig, Stephen Neale, and Charles Parsons (whose notes appear frequently throughout the text) for the help they have given me in finalizing my husband's manuscript. Their most generous gifts of time and attention attest their commitment to my husband and to this book. Arpy Khatchirian, a graduate student who had worked with and for my husband over the past couple of years, was also helpful in the finalizing process.

Marcia Cavell

Preface

Much of the material in this book was contained in or recast from two sets of lectures. The first group of lectures constitute the sixth series of the Dewey Lectures, given at Columbia University in November 1989. The Dewey Lectures were established in 1967 to honor John Dewey. The first of my lectures was "The Structure and Content of Truth," presented on November 9; the second, "Truth and Knowledge," on November 16; and the third, "The Contents of Truth," on November 20. They were published in 1990 as an issue of *The Journal of Philosophy* under the title "The Structure and Content of Truth." All of these lectures have been altered and recast for this volume. The second set of lectures, this time four lectures on "The Problem of Predication," inaugurated the Hermes Lectures at the University of Perugia in May of 2001. Later that same May I gave the first Francesco Sanches Lectures in Lisbon at the invitation of the Instituto de Filosofia da Linguagem; they contained material from the Hermes Lectures. In October of 2001 I delivered the four Hermes Lectures, altered in the light of my ongoing education, at the University of Vienna, and in November of the next year I read the (again altered) lectures to a seminar led by Thorsteinn Gylfason at the University of Iceland in Reykjavik.

Though this is a small book, my indebtedness is large. My Dewey Lectures profited from the helpful suggestions and friendly encouragement of Akeel Bilgrami, Ernest Lepore, Isaac Levi, and W. V. O.

Quine. With the lectures on predication I needed a lot of help, and having, rather uncharacteristically, asked for it, I was generously rewarded. I quizzed each friendly face about two things: who had discussed the problem, and who had solved it. The answers were all to the first question, and were tendered by Akeel Bilgrami, Tyler Burge, Alan Code, Michael Dummett, Michael Frede, Ernie LePore, John McDowell, John McFarlane, Hans Sluga, Barry Stroud, and Bernard Williams. I gave a series of seminars at Berkeley on truth and predication, and as always my students were a wonderful source of questions, criticisms, and suggestions. In Perugia, Carlo Vinti, Antonio Pieretti, and Giancarlo Marchetti ensured that I was well entertained intellectually and otherwise. In Portugal, João Sàágua was my wise and kind mentor. In Vienna, Gabriella Mras provided thoughtfully for my material needs and shored up my historical endeavors, particularly with respect to Frege. My debt to Stephen Neale is great: he introduced the lectures when I first gave them in Perugia, where he stimulated discussion by asking good questions during the discussions that followed the lectures. Subsequently in correspondence and conversation he generously made detailed and extremely useful comments and suggestions. He was once more on board in Iceland. I am most grateful for his friendly interest, support, and sympathetic advice.

Because it has already been published in a journal, and has attracted a certain amount of criticism and comment, I have left the text of the Dewey Lectures pretty much as it was. The chief changes are footnoted. The lectures on predication have been published in Italian in an earlier form. I have modified them here partly to reduce the overlap with the lectures on truth and partly to take advantage of the generous suggestions of the outside readers for Harvard University Press. I must express special gratitude to these three scholars, who carefully read these two sets of lectures when I suggested that they might be combined into a book. The readers, who have agreed to be named, were Charles Parsons, James Higginbotham, and Tyler Burge.

DONALD DAVIDSON

TRUTH AND PREDICATION

Introduction

———

To diagram a few easy sentences.

—F. V. Irish, *Grammar or Analysis by Diagram* (1884)

As a pre-teen scholar I was taught how to diagram a sentence. At the top was the sentence, immediately below which were displayed thick roots (subject and predicate perhaps), which in turn thinned and multiplied as one descended until the smallest parts (usually words) were reached. The whole was like a picture of the descendants of the mother of us all. Those early diagrams foreshadowed the esoteric diagrams, based on the latest syntactic theories, of to-day's linguists.

Diagrams, early and late, are charts of dependencies that may be read either as a way of assembling a proper sentence from a list of parts or of disassembling a sentence into its components. Sentences are concatenations of meaningful parts, as are our utterances and inscriptions of sentences. It is these spoken and written tokens that do the work of communicating information, declaring love, asking directions, issuing orders, or telling a story. Our interest in the parts of sentences, unless the parts themselves are sentences, is derivative; we recognize at once that sentences are the effective linguistic units, while we must figure out or decide what constitutes the meaningful words and particles. Our interest in the parts springs from the need

1

to explain important features of sentences. The lexicographer and the translator want a finite vocabulary from which the endless possible sentences of a language can be constructed; the grammarian is in search of rules for such constructions. The philosopher would like to know the semantic roles of the words which express the concepts she or he would like to understand; the logician requires this semantic knowledge in order to prove that his rules of inference are valid.

This book is mainly concerned with two problems which lie at the heart of semantics: the nature of truth and the semantic role of predicates. The two problems are closely related. We can think of truth as the essential semantic concept with which to begin a top-down analysis of sentences, since truth, or the lack of it, is the most obvious semantic property of sentences, and provides the clearest explanation of what suits sentences to such tasks as expressing judgments or conveying information. Predicates are a part of a bottom-up analysis of sentences, and they are the only indispensable part, since a predicate is the only part of speech that must appear in every sentence. Therefore a grasp of the semantic role of predicates is central to any account of how sentences are articulated.

In the first chapter I discuss the notion, often associated with Tarski's approach, that talk of truth is in some sense redundant, and that truth has no important properties beyond those specified in Tarski's definitions. This chapter ends with a defense of the claim that Tarski's definitions of truth may legitimately be treated as conveying substantive truths about a language, but that in this case there must be more to the concept than Tarski provided. In the second chapter I turn to various attempts to say what more may be involved: I discuss correspondence theories, coherence theories, and theories that in one way or another make truth an epistemic concept. I reject all these kinds of theories. In the third chapter I propose an approach that differs from the rest, one that makes the concept of truth an essential part of the scheme we all employ for understanding, criticizing, explaining, and predicting the thought and action of creatures that think and talk.

I have been chided more than once for leaving out the semantic paradoxes. The honest reason is that I have nothing new to say; I like the proposals of Burge and Parsons. How can I say the concept of truth is so clear? Well, relatively clear. The paradoxes don't intrude in our ordinary talk. Why not? They arise when we try to assign truth values to sentences containing the concept of truth. But sentences are already a long way from most ordinary speech. We don't utter sentences, but rather tokens of sentences. Since communication depends on what we make of the tokens of others, and communication often succeeds, we can normally assume that others mean what we would mean if we uttered those sentences. This is something we can and do check up on, consciously or not, all the time. But it remains the case that we succeed only to a degree (there are many dimensions). Truth, whether of sentences or of utterances, is relative to a language, and we never know exactly what the language is.

It is not my view that therefore the concept of truth is ambiguous. No more, anyway, than in the case of any word. Our words are clear enough in the circumstances in which they have been used. When we test the limits, we are typically not asking "what does it mean?" but "how shall we use it now that these difficulties have come up?"

As for sentences without a truth value, and names without a reference: again, this is a topic on which I do not feel I have any serious and original thoughts. We know the semantic role of names that do refer; it's one of the first things we learned. But this is of no help in deciding whether sentences containing proper names have a truth value. Our intuitions, based on our knowledge of their role when they do refer, prompt one (me) to hold a sentence like 'Zeus does not exist' as true if there is no one who fulfills certain usually adequate properties, and false if someone does. But I intuitively treat the sentences in Homer that recount some of Zeus's sexual misbehavior as neither true nor false. But of course the context is all. I do not mean it is pointless to consider seriously the semantic role of proper names. Just as this book illustrates two different routes into the simplest sentential structures, starting with reflections on the role of proper names might end up doing the same thing. "The Problem of Proper Names" might then have taken the place of "The Problem of Predication."[1]

In the fourth chapter I give a partly historical account of how philosophy has dealt with the problem of predication. The problem has been recognized in one form or another since at least the time of Plato, and many philosophers have attempted to solve it. Yet no one who has faced the problem and proposed an answer has given a satisfactory solution, or so it seems to me. A notable number of contestants have fallen into serious confusion, and several must be admired for having admitted that they were baffled.

The puzzle emerges from the fact that once plausible assignments of semantic roles have been made to the parts of sentences, the parts do not seem to compose a united whole. It is as if a child who has taken a watch apart cannot put it back together. You would think that after repeatedly taking similar watches apart, the deconstructionist would learn to keep track of where the parts came from and how they mesh so that next time reconstruction would be easier. This has not proven to be the case.

The story of the problem of predication, or of the closely related problem of the unity of the proposition, stretches over more than two millennia; it should be told at much greater length than it is here, and by far more knowledgeable historians than I can pretend to be. Portions of the tale have been well and carefully analyzed. What has been missing, so far as I know, is an overview which sug-

---

1. [Davidson had added a note here: "Certainly, for Quine; maybe for Russell."]

gests how long the puzzle has been around, and how the same or similar obstacles, dead ends, and impasses have confronted philosophers again and again. One finds Russell falling into the same trap as Plato, Strawson making a mistake inherited from Aristotle, and many contemporary philosophers of language tumbling into pits dug for them long, or not so long, ago. I am an optimist. I think we can learn to recognize the pattern of errors into which people have been led and can find a reasonable position which retains much of what seemed attractive about the wrong paths while avoiding the pitfalls. The reasonable position, it will become clear, is not one I devised. My contribution, if it is one, is to point out that some of the old puzzles can be put to bed.

Chapter 4 discusses the contributions of Plato and Aristotle. It will be obvious to experts that there is a great deal more to be said about them. I have concentrated on what seem to me the issues that emerge from Plato's theory of forms, and Aristotle's attempt to mend or bend that theory to rid it of the most glaring semantic difficulty.

I then skip to more modern times. My excuse for neglecting the great logicians of the Middle Ages is that Aristotle's logic, impressive as it was, was designed to defeat a reasonable semantics of predicates, since terms like 'all men,' 'some horses,' and 'no member' are semantically and logically indigestible. Failure to plug this vast historical hole in my account is mitigated by the existence of Peter Geach's book *Reference and Generality,* which does much to fill the gap. Geach's wonderful book traces the struggles of logicians, medieval and modern, to cope with quantification and predication, and in effect concludes, correctly in my opinion, that it was not until Frege that a satisfactory solution to the problem of predication was possible. But, unlike Geach, I do not think that Frege himself offered a satisfactory solution. Nevertheless, *Reference and Generality* is a model of the kind of book I wish I had the wit and wisdom to have written about predication.

In Chapter 5 I discuss a number of failed attempts to explain the semantic role of predicates. Bertrand Russell and the question of the unity of the proposition dominate the first part of the chapter. Russell was uneasy about the dual role of predicates, since analysis seemed to demand that predicates denote universals or relations, but this destroyed their unifying function and left open the question of what glued the analyzed parts of sentences together. Strawson was apparently not bothered by this problem, and embraced the duality. This provoked a debate with Quine in which Quine makes a pregnant suggestion that is not developed. The chapter ends with a discussion of a treatment of predicates by Wilfrid Sellars, a treatment which he says was inspired by Wittgenstein.

Chapter 6 emphasizes the close relation between predication and truth. Consideration of Frege's and Church's arguments against facts, correspondence to which might yield an analysis of truth, leads to Frege's famous proposal that predicates be considered functional expressions. In this connection I describe Dummett's proposed revision of Frege, but in the end I reject both Frege's admittedly brilliant project and Dummett's attempt to improve on it.

The final chapter lists in summary form the moves that have proved to lead to dead ends, and at least some of the desiderata of a satisfactory account of predication. Not surprisingly, I think that the best approach is some version of Tarski's truth definitions, though for several reasons this is not a conclusion with which everyone will be happy, and probably no one will be completely content with it.

CHAPTER 1

Theories of Truth

Nothing in the world, no object or event, would be true or false if there were not thinking creatures. John Dewey drew two conclusions: that access to truth could not be a special prerogative of philosophy, and that truth must have essential connections with human interests. He was contemptuous of the philosophical tradition that viewed truth as correspondence between thought and a reality inaccessible to experimental research and ordinary practice. He believed this picture of truth was designed to serve the thesis that philosophers possess a privileged technique for achieving a form of knowledge different from, and superior to, science. Dewey wrote that

> the profuseness of attestations to supreme devotion to truth on the part of philosophy is matter to arouse suspicion. For it has usually been a preliminary to the claim of being a peculiar organ of access to highest and ultimate truth. Such it is not. . . . Truth is a collection of truths; and these constituent truths are in the keeping of the best available methods of inquiry and testing as to matters-of-fact; methods, which are, when collected under a single name, science. As to truth, then, philosophy has no pre-eminent status.[1]

1. John Dewey, *Experience and Nature* (New York: Dover, 1958), p. 410.

Dewey's aim was to bring truth, and with it the pretensions of philosophers, down to earth. We may with justice feel that Dewey confused the question of what sort of concept truth is with the question of what kinds of truth there are. But it is clear that the two issues are related, since what falls under the concept obviously depends on what the concept is. And the idea of ensuring that the domain of truth can be convincingly brought within the scope of human powers by cutting the concept down to size is hardly unique to Dewey; Dewey saw himself as sharing the views of C. I. Lewis, Peirce, and William James in this matter, and in one way or another the basic theme reappears today in the writings of Hilary Putnam, Richard Rorty, and many others.

Those who wish to debunk or deflate the concept of truth often start by rejecting any hint of the correspondence theory, but Dewey saw no harm in the idea of correspondence as long as it was properly understood. "Truth means, as a matter of course, agreement, correspondence, of idea and fact," he said, but immediately went on, "but what do agreement, correspondence mean?"[2] He answered, "The idea is true which works in leading us to what it purports," and he quotes James with approval:

> Any idea that will carry us prosperously from any one part of experience to any other part, linking things satisfactorily, working securely, simplifying, saving labor, is true for just so much, true in so far forth.[3]

2. John Dewey, *Essays in Experimental Logic* (New York: Dover, 1953), p. 304.

3. William James, *Pragmatism* (New York: Longmans & Green, 1907), p. 58. Elsewhere, in *Logic: The Theory of Inquiry* (New York: Holt, 1938), p. 58, Dewey says: "The best definition of *truth* from the logical standpoint which is known to me is that of Peirce: 'The opinion which is fated to be ultimately agreed to by all who investigate is what we mean by the truth.'" But usually Dewey was closer to James: ideas, theories, are true if they are "instrumental to an active reorganization of the given environment, to a removal of some specific trouble and perplexity . . . The hypothesis that works is the *true* one." John Dewey, *Reconstruction in Philosophy* (New York: Holt, 1920), p. 156.

Probably few philosophers are now tempted by these sweeping formulations. But the problem the pragmatists were addressing—the problem of how to relate truth to human desires, beliefs, intentions, and the use of language—seems to me the right one to concentrate on in thinking about truth. It also seems to me this problem is not much nearer a solution today than it was in Dewey's day.

To see this as a main problem about truth, or indeed as a problem at all, is to assume that the concept of truth is related in important ways to human attitudes—something it is not uncommon to doubt. It is not uncommon, in fact, to doubt whether the concept of truth is of any serious philosophic importance at all. Rorty captures Dewey's intention of removing truth from a realm so exalted only philosophers could hope to attain it when he introduces his *Consequences of Pragmatism* with the words:

> The essays in this book are attempts to draw consequences from a pragmatist theory about truth. This theory says that truth is not the sort of thing one should expect to have a philosophically interesting theory about . . . there is no interesting work to be done in this area.[4]

But it seems to me Rorty misses half the point of Dewey's attitude toward the concept of truth: Dewey says that *truths* are not in general the special province of philosophy; but he also insists that *truth* is what works. This is not the same as the thesis that there is nothing interesting to be said about the concept of truth. Dewey found plenty that was interesting to say about what works.

Rorty has compared my views on the nature of truth with Dewey's.[5] I find much of what he has to say on this topic congenial,

4. Richard Rorty, *Consequences of Pragmatism* (Minneapolis: University of Minnesota Press, 1982), pp. xiii–xiv.

5. Richard Rorty, "Pragmatism, Davidson, and Truth," in *Truth and Interpretation,* ed. E. Lepore (New York: Blackwell, 1986), pp. 333–355. See also his "Representation, Social Practice, and Truth," *Philosophical Studies* 30 (1988): 215–228. [Note added by Davidson, 2003: "Rorty and I have continued to converse on the topic of truth. Our exchange in *Rorty and His Critics*, ed. Robert Brandom (Oxford: Blackwell, 2000), pp. 65–108, is a recent sample."]

and I think he is right that in a general way I share Dewey's attitude toward truth. In one respect, though, a respect on which I just touched, Rorty may have us both wrong; as I read him, Dewey thought that once truth was brought down to earth there were philosophically important and instructive things to say about its connections with human attitudes, connections partly constitutive of the concept of truth. This is also my view, though I do not think Dewey had the connections right.

Rorty correctly notes the fundamental role I assign to Alfred Tarski's work as providing a way of discussing the understanding of language, and he sees clearly that for me this is related to the rejection of a representational picture of language and the idea that truth consists in the accurate mirroring of facts. These are matters to which I shall turn presently.

Dewey's view is deflationary only in its rejection of philosophy's inflated pretensions to be privy to foundational truths denied to other disciplines. Rorty goes much further when he derides the philosophical interest in the concept of truth. This is not an entirely new attitude. Some version of the redundancy theory must have arisen early. The redundancy theory best fits phrases like 'It is true that' or 'It is a fact that' when prefixed to a sentence. Such phrases may be regarded as truth-functional sentential connectives which, when added to a true sentence, yield a true sentence, and when added to a false sentence, yield a false sentence. These connectives would then function exactly like double negation (when negation is classically understood). At least so far as cognitive content and truth conditions are concerned, such appendages are redundant.

Frank Ramsey seems to have thought that all uses of the concept of truth are like this. He says: "'It is true that Caesar was murdered' means no more than that Caesar was murdered."[6] He then considers cases like 'Everything he says is true' from which reference to

6. F. P. Ramsey, "Facts and Propositions," in *The Foundations of Mathematics* (New York: Humanities Press, 1950), pp. 138–155; p. 143.

truth is not so easily eliminated, and suggests that, if we restrict ourselves to propositions of the form *aRb,* we could render 'Everything he *says is* true' as 'For all *a, R, b,* if he *says aRb,* then *aRb.*' Ramsey adds that, if all forms of proposition are included, things get more complicated, "but not essentially different."[7] Although Ramsey does not always clearly distinguish between propositions and sentences, or the use of sentences and their mention, one gets the impression that, if Ramsey had carried out the "more complicated" analysis, he might have ended up with something much like one of Tarski's truth definitions. In any case, Ramsey thought he had said enough to show that "there is really no separate problem of truth but merely a linguistic muddle."[8]

Ramsey was wrong if he thought the truth-functional-connective analysis of the use of 'true' could be directly applied to sentences like 'Everything he says is true,' for in the former case the truth phrase is viewed as a connective, whereas in the latter case it must be treated as a predicate and, if we follow Tarski, it must belong to a different language from the language of the sentences of which it is predicated. It might be possible to treat phrases like 'It is true that' as predicates of propositions rather than as sentential connectives, but again the redundancy would be far less manifest than Ramsey claimed.

Many philosophers have nevertheless regarded Tarski's work as essentially a matter of straightening out Ramsey's insight. W. V. Quine, for example, writes: "To say that the statement 'Brutus killed Caesar' is true . . . is in effect simply to say that Brutus killed Caesar," and he tells us, in a footnote, to see Tarski for the "classic development" of this theme.[9] Putnam maintains that Rorty and

7. Ibid., p. 143.
8. Ibid., p. 142. P. F. Strawson says much the same in his famous debate with J. L. Austin, in "Truth," *Proceedings of the Aristotelian Society,* Supplementary Volume 24 (1950): 129–156.
9. W. V. Quine, *Word and Object* (Cambridge, Mass.: MIT Press, 1960), p. 24.

Quine share this view of truth. According to Putnam, Rorty and Quine believe that "to call a sentence 'true' is not to ascribe a property, truth, to a sentence; it is just another way of asserting the sentence."[10] (He adds that this is called the "disquotational view"— "in the jargon of Davidsonian philosophers of language." Maybe so, but then I am not a Davidsonian, for I am not tempted to refer to Tarski's truth definitions as "disquotational." In any case, Putnam is not endorsing this thesis; he is attacking it as "purely formal" and "empty.")

It is not clear to me whether Putnam thinks Tarski's work on truth is no more than a technical improvement on what is basically a redundancy theory, but others have certainly taken this line. Stephen Leeds has suggested that the "usefulness" or importance of the concept of truth might just consist in this, that it gives us a way to say things like "Most of our beliefs are true," where we want to talk of, or perhaps assert, an infinite or otherwise unlistable set of sentences. Ramsey did not explain how to do this; Tarski did.[11] Paul Horwich, like Leeds, considers Tarski to be a redundancy theorist; Horwich is persuaded that, despite our intuition that truth is a central and important concept, "the notion of truth was completely captured by Tarski."[12] This idea, that Tarski did all that could be done for the concept of truth, Horwich calls the deflationary theory of truth.

Although he does not agree with Horwich that truth as Tarski defined it specifies truth conditions adequate to an account of what language users know, Scott Soames concurs in calling Tarski's approach to truth deflationary, and like Horwich he thinks that when

10. Hilary Putnam, "A Comparison of Something with Something Else," *New Literary History* 17 (1985–86): 61–79; p. 62.

11. Stephen Leeds, "Theories of Reference and Truth," *Erkenntnis* 13 (1978): 111–130.

12. Paul Horwich, "Three Forms of Realism," *Synthese* 51 (1982): 181–201; p. 192.

it comes to explicating the concept of truth, we should not ask for anything more, aside from the application of truth to propositions, etc.[13]

Hartry Field, in a useful article, explores the case for a deflationary concept of truth, and shows how hard it would be to go beyond it. He explains what he means by calling a theory of truth "deflationary" in approximately the way Horwich does: truth is disquotational and nothing more; but he is less certain than Horwich that Tarski should (or must) be seen as a disquotationist, though he believes Tarski's work can be appropriated by the disquotationist.[14] Michael Williams, who declares himself a deflationist, has recently characterized the view this way: deflationists

> think that when we have pointed to certain formal features of the truth-predicate (notably its 'disquotational' feature) and explained why it is useful to have a predicate like this (e.g. as a device for asserting infinite conjunctions), we have said just about everything there is to be said about truth.[15]

How plausible are these various deflationary theories of truth?[16] If we restrict the redundancy theory to occurrences of 'true' as part of a truth-functional sentential connective (as in 'It is true that snow

13. Scott Soames, "What Is a Theory of Truth?" *Journal of Philosophy* 81 (1984): 411–429.

14. Hartry Field, "The Deflationary Conception of Truth," in *Fact, Science, and Morality,* ed. C. Wright and G. MacDonald (New York: Blackwell, 1987), pp. 55–117.

15. Michael Williams, "Epistemological Realism and the Basis of Skepticism," *Mind* 97 (1988): 415–439; p. 424. See also Michael Williams, "Do We (Epistemologists) Need a Theory of Truth?" *Philosophical Topics* 54 (1986): 223–242.

16. [Davidson wanted to add that he discussed Horwich's *Truth* (Oxford: Blackwell, 1990) and Hartry Field's "Deflationist Views on Meaning and Content," *Mind* 103 (1994): 249–285, in his (Davidson's) "The Folly of Trying to Define Truth," *Journal of Philosophy* 93 (1996), 263–278.]

is white'), then it is clear that such uses play only a small role in our talk of truth; this cannot be the whole story. Can disquotational theories do better? Tarski's truth definitions are disquotational in this sense: given the definition (and set theory and formal syntax), and given a sentence in the form "'Snow is white' is true," we can prove that the sentence 'Snow is white' is equivalent. Thus, the sentence in which 'Snow is white' was only mentioned is provably equivalent to the sentence 'Snow is white' itself; the original "'Snow is white'" has been stripped of its quotation marks; removing the quotation marks canceled out, so to speak, the truth predicate. And even when we cannot remove the quotation marks because there are no quotation marks to remove (as in 'Everything he said was true' or 'A valid rule of inference guarantees that from true premises only true conclusions follow'), Tarski has shown us how to get rid of the truth predicate, since it has been explicitly defined.[17] This makes clear that Tarski's truth definitions are not strictly disquotational, since they do not depend on stripping the quotation marks from individual sentences in order to eliminate truth predicates. Still less do they depend on using the actual sentences said to be true to effect the elimination; this is obvious when the definition of truth for one language is given in another. One cannot find an English equivalent of the English sentence "'Schnee ist weiss' is true (in German)" simply by removing the quotation marks from "'Schnee ist weiss.'"

Still, the fact remains that Tarski's methods allow us to replace, in any context in which it occurs, the truth predicates he defines, and the replacement leaves no explicitly semantical predicates in its wake; in this respect, his truth predicates are like the sentential connective 'it is true that,' which may be removed by simple deletion. It

17. This point, often credited to Leeds, was made by Tarski in "The Semantic Conception of Truth," *Philosophy and Phenomenological Research* 4 (1944): 341–376; p. 359. Tarski also notes that mere disquotation cannot eliminate the word 'true' from sentences like 'The first sentence written by Plato is true.'

is presumably this feature which leads Putnam to say that, according to such theories, truth is not a property. (This cannot be exactly right as applied to Tarski's truth definitions, however. Tarski's truth predicates are legitimate predicates, with extensions that no predicate in the object language has. But one sees the point of Putnam's remark.) Putnam concludes that Tarski's truth predicates have nothing to do with semantics or the common conception of truth: "As a philosophical account of truth, Tarski's theory fails as badly as it is possible for an account to fail."[18]

What is clear is that Tarski did not define the concept of truth, even as applied to sentences. Tarski showed how to define a truth predicate for each of a number of well-behaved languages, but his definitions do not, of course, tell us what these predicates have in common. Put a little differently: he defined various predicates of the form 's is true in L', each applicable to a single language, but he failed to define a predicate of the form 's is true in L' for variable 'L'. The point was made by Max Black[19] and subsequently by Dummett;[20] but of course Tarski had made this thunderously clear from the start by proving that no such single predicate could be defined in a consistent language, given his assumptions concerning truth predicates. Given those constraints, there was never any chance that he could give a general definition of the concept of truth, even for sentences. If we consider the application of the concept of truth to beliefs and related phenomena like claims and assertions, it is obvious in a further way that Tarski did not attempt a really general definition. Considering how evident it is that Tarski did not give a general definition of truth, and the fact that perhaps his most important result was that it could not be done along lines that would

18. Putnam, "A Comparison of Something with Something Else," p. 64.
19. Max Black, *Language and Philosophy* (Ithaca: Cornell University Press, 1949), p. 104.
20. Michael Dummett, "Truth," in *Truth and Other Enigmas* (London: Duckworth, 1978), pp. 1–24.

satisfy him, it is remarkable how much effort some critics have put into the attempt to persuade us that Tarski failed to provide such a definition.

Dummett says in the Preface to *Truth and Other Enigmas* that the "fundamental contention" of his early article "Truth" was that any form of the redundancy theory (and he includes Tarski's truth definitions in this category) must be false because no such theory can capture the point of introducing a truth predicate. This can be seen, he argues, from the fact that, if we have a Tarskian truth definition for a language that we do not understand,

> we shall have no idea of the point of introducing the predicate . . .
> unless . . . we already know in advance what the point of the predi-
> cate so defined is supposed to be. But, if we do know in advance the
> point of introducing the predicate "true" then we know something
> about the concept of truth expressed by that predicate which is not
> embodied in that . . . truth definition.[21]

Dummett adds that "although this contention was so obvious when formulated I believe that it was worth stating at the time." He is right: the contention was obvious, and was worth stating, at least to me.[22] The application to theories of meaning is important, but the issue is more general: Tarski knew he could not give a general definition of truth, and so there was no formal way he could capture "the point" of introducing truth predicates, whether that point

21. Dummett, *Truth and Other Enigmas,* pp. xx–xxi.

22. My confusion on this point is most apparent in "Truth and Meaning," in *Inquiries into Truth and Interpretation,* 2nd ed. (New York: Oxford University Press, 2001). My mistake was to think we could *both* take a Tarski truth defini- tion as telling us all we need to know about truth *and* use the definition to de- scribe an actual language. But even in the same essay I (inconsistently) discussed how to tell that such a definition applied to a language. I soon recognized the error. (See the Introduction, pp. xiv–xv, and other essays in *Inquiries into Truth and Interpretation.*)

concerned the connection between truth and meaning or between truth and some other concept or concepts.

Dummett and others have attempted in various ways to make the slow-witted among us appreciate the failure of Tarski's truth predicates to capture completely the concept of truth. The central difficulty, as we have seen, is due simply to the fact that Tarski does not tell us how to apply the concept to a new case, whether the new case is a new language or a word newly added to a language (these are really the same point, put both ways by Dummett and the second way by Hartry Field).[23] This feature of Tarski's definitions can in turn easily be traced to the fact that they depend on giving the extension or reference of the basic predicates or names by enumerating cases: a definition given in this way can provide no clue for the next or general case.

A number of criticisms of, or comments on, Tarski's treatment of truth depend on the enumerative aspect of his definitions. One such is the claim that Tarski's definitions cannot explain why, if the word 'snow' had meant 'coal', the sentence 'Snow is white' would have been true if and only if snow had been black. Putnam and Soames both make the point, but for Putnam it is a criticism, while for Soames it illustrates the folly of expecting much from a theory or definition of truth.[24] Another complaint is that Tarski's definitions do not establish the connection between truth and meaning that many philosophers hold to be essential. (Again, for Putnam this shows there is something basically wrong with Tarski's conception of truth; for Soames it is one more example of the laudably deflationary aspect of Tarski's definitions.) A closely related comment is that Tarski does not relate truth to the use or users of language (Field, Putnam, Soames, Dummett). Whatever the value of these remarks may be, it is worth keeping in mind that they all trace back

23. Hartry Field, "Tarski's Theory of Truth," *Journal of Philosophy* 69 (1972): 347–375.

24. See my "The Folly of Trying to Define Truth."

to the same simple feature of Tarski's work: by employing a finite and exhaustive list of basic cases in the course of defining satisfaction (in terms of which truth is defined), he necessarily failed to specify how to go on to further cases.

Despite the limitations that have been identified or imagined to exist in Tarski's work on truth, a number of philosophers, as we have seen, have endorsed that work as embracing all of truth's essential features. These philosophers include Rorty, Leeds, Michael Williams, Horwich, Soames, and, according to Putnam, Quine; also, according to Rorty, me.

I do not belong on this list, however. The basic argument, which was intended to reveal Tarski as a deflationist, can be taken in two ways: as showing that he did not capture essential aspects of the concept of truth, or as showing that the concept of truth is not as deep and interesting as many have thought.[25] Like Dummett and Putnam, I think we must take it in the first of these two ways. The reason is plain. Tarski has not told us what his truth definitions have in common. Unless we are prepared to say there is no single concept of truth (even as applied to sentences), but only a number of different concepts for which we use the same word, we have to conclude that there is more to the concept of truth, something absolutely basic, which Tarski's definitions do not touch. What is mildly puzzling is that some philosophers who appeal to the "basic argument" (to show that Tarski's truth definitions are deflationary) also accept a deflationary theory, because at the same time that argument shows, as I have said, that there is more to the concept of

25. The first attitude stands out in Putnam's remark that the property Tarski defined is not "even doubtfully or dubiously 'close' to the property of truth. It just isn't truth at all." Putnam, "A Comparison of Something with Something Else," p. 64. Soames represents the second view: "What does seem right about Tarski's approach is its deflationary character." But "Tarski's notion of truth has nothing to do with semantic interpretation or understanding." Scott Soames, "What Is a Theory of Truth?" *Journal of Philosophy* 81 (1984): 411–429; pp. 429, 424.

truth than is captured by any deflationary theory. If the argument is sound, it shows that definitions like Tarski's, or theories built on the same lines, cannot capture the concept of truth.

There is a further claim or assumption about Tarski's work which, though it is often run together with some of the points just rehearsed, deserves separate discussion. The theme is that, if we accept one of Tarski's truth definitions, then statements that ought, if truth were properly characterized, to be empirical statements are turned into truths of logic. Thus, according to Putnam, a sentence like "'Schnee ist weiss' is true (in German) if and only if snow is white" ought to be a substantive truth about German, but if for the predicate '*s* is true (in German)' we substitute a predicate defined in Tarski's style, the apparent substantive truth becomes a truth of logic.[26] It is easy to see that whatever there is to this argument depends on the same feature of Tarski's method that I have been discussing: if the extension of a predicate is defined by listing the things to which it applies, applying the predicate to an item on the list will yield a statement equivalent to a logical truth. (For technical reasons, this is an oversimplified explanation of this aspect of Tarski's method when the object language includes quantifiers, etc. The force of the point remains.)[27] This seems to be Putnam's main reason for saying that Tarski failed "as badly as it is possible to fail" in giving a philosophical account of truth. Soames may be thinking along the same lines when he maintains that the only way to defend Tarski's philosophical interpretation of his work is to reject the demand that applications of his truth and satisfaction predi-

26. For versions of this argument, see Putnam, "A Comparison of Something with Something Else," and "On Truth," in *How Many Questions?* ed. Leigh Cauman et al. (Indianapolis: Hackett, 1983), pp. 35–56.

27. For the development of this theme, see the works of Putnam cited in note 24; see also Soames, "What Is a Theory of Truth?" and John Etchemendy, "Tarski on Truth and Logical Consequence," *Journal of Symbolic Logic* 53 (1988): 51–79.

cates have empirical content. To meet the demand would, Soames says, be "incompatible" with Tarski's work.[28]

The argument is spelled out at some length by John Etchemendy.[29] According to Etchemendy, Tarski's goal was to formulate predicates with two properties: first, they should be related in a specific way to the intuitive concept of truth, and second, they should be guaranteed, as far as possible, against the threat of paradox and inconsistency. The first condition was met by devising a concept that could easily be shown to apply to all and only the true sentences of a language. The relation to the intuitive concept of truth is made manifest by Convention-T. Convention-T requires that the truth predicate 's is true in L' for a language L be so defined as to entail, for every sentence s of L, a theorem of the form 's is true in L if and only if p', when 's' is replaced by a systematic description of s and p is replaced by a translation of s into the language of the theory. Let us call these theorems T-sentences. The predicate in T-sentences, 's is true in L', is a one-place predicate; the 'L' is not a variable, but the name or description of a particular language and an undetachable part of the predicate. The relation to the ordinary concept of truth is apparent from the fact that T-sentences remain true if for the Tarski-style truth predicate we substitute the English predicate 's is true in L'. (This is a two-place predicate: we can substitute names or descriptions of other languages for 'L'.) The demand that the truth predicate should not threaten to introduce inconsistencies into the theory or language is met by giving an explicit definition of the predicate using no semantic concepts; thus, any challenge to consistency that such concepts might present has been avoided. If the metalanguage is consistent before the introduction of the truth predicate, it is guaranteed to remain so after the introduction.

28. Soames, "What Is a Theory of Truth?", p. 425.
29. Etchemendy, "Tarski on Truth and Logical Consequence."

T-sentences containing Tarski's truth predicates *seem* to convey substantive facts about the object language, namely, that its sentences are true under conditions specified by the T-sentence (e.g., "'Schnee ist weiss' is true in German if and only if snow is white"), but in fact, says Etchemendy, "they carry no information about the semantic properties of [the] language, *not even about the truth-conditions of its sentences.*"[30] The reason for this is that T-sentences are truths of logic, and thus cannot tell us anything logic alone cannot tell us. T-sentences are truths of logic because they follow from Tarski's definitions, and these are merely stipulations; we are misled because of "the ease with which we read substantive content into what is intended as a stipulative definition, the ease with which we replace the 'if and only if' of definition with the 'if and only if' of axioms or theorems."[31] If we want to state substantive facts about a language, we must substitute in T-sentences and elsewhere a predicate that conveys something like the intuitive concept of truth. If we do this, "the claims we make will sometimes look strikingly like clauses" in Tarski's definitions and (if correct) will yield genuine information about the semantic properties of a language.

But—and this is Etchemendy's central message—the two enterprises—of defining truth according to Tarski's aims, and of providing a formal but substantive semantic account of a language—are not only totally different enterprises, but are in "quite direct opposition to one another. . . . For without setting aside Tarski's principal goal, there is a sense in which semantics simply cannot be done." The difference between the two is that the first demands a predicate that can be eliminated without remainder from all contexts, while the second requires a "fixed, metatheoretical" notion of truth. Employing the second concept would directly defeat the point of Tarski's project. Thus, the relation between Tarski's in-

30. Ibid., p. 57 (emphasis in the original).
31. Ibid., p. 58.

tended and successful achievement, on the one hand, and the project of supplying a way of describing the semantics of interpreted languages, on the other, is "little more than a fortuitous accident."[32]

Putnam, Soames, and Etchemendy agree that Tarski's T-sentences only appear to state empirical truths about a language; they are in fact "tautologies" (Putnam). The three differ in their appraisals of the thesis on which they agree: Putnam thinks what Tarski defined "just isn't truth at all";[33] Soames and Etchemendy hold that Tarski did what he set out to do. Soames holds that Tarski was right to give a deflationary account of truth, while Etchemendy thinks empirical semantics is a legitimate study which Tarski was not pursuing. How should we think about these claims? One thing is certain: Tarski did not agree with these assessments of his results. In "The Semantic Conception of Truth,"[34] there is a section headed "Conformity of the Semantic Conception of Truth with Philosophical and Common-Sense Usage." Let me quote from it:

> As far as my own opinion is concerned, I do not have any doubts that our formulation does conform to the intuitive content of that of Aristotle . . . some doubts have been expressed whether the semantic conception does reflect the notion of truth in its common-sense and everyday usage. I clearly realize . . . that the common meaning of the word *"true"*—as that of any other word of everyday language—is to some extent vague . . . Hence . . . every solution of this problem implies necessarily a certain deviation from the practice of everyday language. In spite of all this, I happen to believe that the semantic conception does conform to a considerable extent with the common-sense usage.[35]

In setting up his problem, Tarski does not distance himself from the project of characterizing concepts that can be used as the ordi-

32. Ibid., pp. 52–53.
33. Putnam, "A Comparison of Something with Something Else," p. 64.
34. Tarski, "The Semantic Conception of Truth," pp. 341–375.
35. Ibid., p. 360.

nary semantic concepts are used—concepts that express, as he says, "connexions between the expressions of a language and the objects and states of affairs referred to by these expressions."[36] He does not aim, he says, to assign a new meaning to an old word, but to "catch hold of the actual meaning of an old notion."[37] In other words, he is quite explicit that he did not intend his definitions to be purely stipulative.

Tarski describes his project as "The Establishment of Scientific Semantics," and he says that "semantic concepts express certain relations between objects (and states of affairs) referred to in the language discussed and expressions of the language referring to these objects."[38] He regards the truth of a sentence as its "correspondence with reality." Tarski regards these characterizations of semantic concepts as "vague," but clearly they would be totally wrong if semantic concepts had no empirical application. When Tarski requires that his definitions be "materially adequate and in accordance with ordinary usage," he argues that Convention-T is just what assures us that the condition is met. The argument is this: given a language we understand, an interpreted language such as English, we recognize as true all sentences of the form "'Snow is white' is true if and only if snow is white." Tarski calls such sentences "partial definitions" of truth. Obviously, a definition that entails all such sentences will have the same extension (for the specified language) as the intuitive concept of truth with which we started. To admit this is to count T-sentences as having empirical content; otherwise Convention-T would have no point, nor would Tarski's insistence that he is interested in defining truth only for interpreted languages.

We must conclude, I think, that if Etchemendy, Soames, and

---

36. Alfred Tarski, "The Establishment of Scientific Semantics," in *Logic, Semantics, Metamathematics,* ed. J. H. Woodger (New York: Oxford University Press, 1956), pp. 401–408; p. 401.

37. Tarski, "The Semantic Conception of Truth," p. 341.

38. Tarski, "The Establishment of Scientific Semantics," pp. 403–404.

Putnam are right, Tarski mistook his own aim and the nature of his accomplishment. Yet surprisingly little needs to be done to reconcile Tarski with Etchemendy. Etchemendy allows, of course, that "Tarski introduced precisely the mathematical techniques needed for an illuminating account of the semantic properties of certain simple languages," and "getting from a Tarskian definition of truth to a substantive account of the semantic properties of the object language may involve as little as the reintroduction of a primitive notion of truth."[39] The trick is just to add to Tarski's definition of a truth predicate for a language L (say, 's is true$_L$') the remark that Tarski's predicate holds for all and only the true sentences of L. Here, of course, the word 'true' expresses the real-life, substantive, undefined concept we need for serious semantics. Let us call this remark the *truth axiom*.

The first thing to notice is that, if the language was consistent before we added the truth axiom, the truth axiom cannot make it inconsistent as long as we do not formally endow our new predicate with any properties. It can *have* all sorts of interesting properties and no formal harm will be done if the properties are not explicitly entered in the theory; and no informal harm will be done if the additional properties do not lead to contradiction.

Adding the truth axiom is, from a formal point of view, harmless; it is also pointless. For we can just as well regard Tarski's truth predicate 's is true$_L$' as having the properties of our real-life predicate 's is true in L', as long as those properties do not create inconsistencies. The objection to this thought is that we can no longer feel confident that, if we were to specify all the properties of the real-life predicate, inconsistencies might not result; we do not know exactly what our truth predicate means. The "definition" of truth is no longer a purely stipulative definition.

Consider a formalized object language and a metalanguage ex-

39. Etchemendy, "Tarski on Truth and Logical Consequence," pp. 59–60.

Theories of Truth · 25

actly like those described by Tarski in sections 2 and 3 of "The Concept of Truth in Formalized Languages."[40] Now add to the metalanguage Tarski's definitions leading up to and including the definition of truth; but do not call them definitions, and think of them as employing empirically significant expressions suitable for describing the semantics of the object language (which has been interpreted as about the calculus of classes by Tarski). According to Etchemendy, the difference between this new system and Tarski's original is extreme: the new system correctly describes the semantics of the object language, while Tarski's system merely defines a predicate that cannot be used to assert anything, true or false, about any particular interpreted language. Tarski's definitions turn the entailed T-sentences into logical truths; the new system leaves them as instructive remarks about the truth conditions of sentences. But this mighty change does not touch the formal system in any way; it is a change in how we describe the system, not in the system itself. If Tarski's system is consistent, so is the new one.

The entire issue turns, then, on how we regard definitions. Some definitions clearly are intended to introduce new words; others aim to express substantive truths of one sort or another. As we have seen, Tarski did not intend his definitions to foist a new meaning on an old term, but to "catch hold of the actual meaning of an old notion."[41]

We should now glance back at the theme, to be found not only in Etchemendy, but also in Putnam and Soames, that Tarski's truth

40. Alfred Tarski, "The Concept of Truth in Formalized Languages," in *Logic, Semantics, Metamathematics*, ed. Woodger, pp. 152–278.
41. Etchemendy suggests that the "if and only if" of a definition does not have the same meaning as the "if and only if" of a substantive claim, but I do not think this remark can be taken seriously because the difference makes no difference at all within the system, and if we were to mark the supposed difference by introducing different symbols, the rules of inference in the system would have to be altered. Etchemendy says his suggestion was not intended to be taken seriously (private conversation).

definitions cannot have anything to do with the semantics or interpretation of actual languages because, given his definitions, the relevant theorems (e.g., the T-sentences) are logical truths. In fact, they
are logical truths only on the assumption that Tarski's truth definitions are purely stipulative, that they tell us everything there is to
know about the predicates he defines. There is no reason to accept
this assumption. A simple analogy will make this clear. Suppose we
offer as a definition of the predicate 'x is a solar planet' the following: x is a solar planet if and only if x is just one of the following:
Mercury, Venus, Earth, Mars, Jupiter, Saturn, Uranus, Neptune,
Pluto. This entails the P-sentence 'Neptune is a solar planet.' Is
this last a logical truth? One may as well say so if our definition
is purely stipulative, otherwise not. The question of whether it is
purely stipulative is not one that can be answered by studying the
formal system; it concerns the intentions of the person making the
definition. If we were simply presented with the defining sentence,
we could hardly fail to notice that, if we interpret the words in more
or less the usual way, it expresses a substantive truth. By appeal to
Convention-T, Tarski invites us to notice an analogous feature of
his truth definitions.

What should we conclude about how Tarski intended us to take
his definitions? The indications may seem ambiguous. On the one
hand, we have his repeated and explicit claim that he wished to,
and thought he had, "caught the actual meaning" of the intuitive
concept of truth, so far as this was possible; on the other hand, he
clearly depended on the fact that his definitions allowed the elimination of all explicitly semantic vocabulary to guarantee that his
concept would not introduce inconsistencies into an otherwise consistent language. But does this show that Tarski was confused? I
think not. Here is a way of viewing the matter.

Tarski's definitions endow his truth predicates with properties
that ensure that they define the class of true sentences in a language.
If the predicates have no further properties, we know they will

not breed inconsistencies. This makes the predicates useful for certain purposes. If we think of the truth predicates as having further unspecified properties, we cannot be sure those properties will not make trouble if they are made explicit. But there is nothing to prevent us from working within Tarski's systems while acknowledging that the truth predicates may have further essential properties, as long as we make no use of the unspecified properties. In this way, we can take full advantage of Tarski's technical achievement while not treating the contents of his theories as "empty" or "merely" formal.

To view Tarski's work in this light is to admit that there is a clear sense in which he did not define the concept of truth, even for particular languages. He defined the class of true sentences by giving the extension of the truth predicate, but he did not give the meaning. This follows the moment we decide that T-sentences have empirical content, for this implies that there is more to the concept of truth than Tarski's definition tells us. My contention is not that Tarski may after all have captured a substantial concept of truth, but that we are not necessarily confused if we interpret his formal systems as empirical theories about languages. By doing so, we avoid two potentially crippling theses about truth, theses which, as we have seen, are fairly common today. One—which we might call Scylla—is that Tarski's work is largely unrelated to the concept of truth as we ordinarily understand it, so that, if we want to study the semantics of interpreted languages, we must take another tack. The other—Charybdis—is the thesis that, although Tarski's version of truth is merely disquotational, it says all there is to say about the concept of truth.

My own view is that Tarski has told us much of what we want to know about the concept of truth, and that there must be more. There must be more because there is no indication in Tarski's formal work of what it is that his various truth predicates have in common, and this must be part of the content of the concept. It is not enough to point to Convention-T as that indication, for it does not speak to the question of how we know that a theory of truth for a language is correct. The concept of truth has essential connections with the concepts of belief and meaning, but these connections are untouched by Tarski's work. It is here that we should expect to uncover what we miss in Tarski's characterizations of truth predicates.

What Tarski has done for us is show in detail how to describe the kind of pattern truth must make, whether in language or in thought. What we need to do now is to say how to identify the presence of such a pattern or structure in the behavior of people.

CHAPTER 2

What More Is There to Truth?

If there were no more to be known about the concept of truth than we can learn from Tarski's definitions of truth predicates, we would have no clear use for the concept of truth aside from the minor convenience of its disquotational function, since Tarski has shown how to eliminate such predicates without semantic residue. Any connection of truth with meaning or belief would be moot. If we think of Tarski's definitions as purely stipulative, the theorems such predicates allow us to prove, in particular the T-sentences, are truths of logic; unless we read more into the truth predicates than the definitions provide, these theorems cannot, therefore, express empirical truths about the sentences of any language, and cannot be taken to give the truth conditions of such sentences.

Tarski never claimed that his truth predicates did more than pick out the set of true sentences in particular languages. He certainly did not think he had defined a general truth predicate, nor did he aim to exceed the limits of extensionality. Capturing meaning, as distinguished from extension, was no part of his project. Nor did it matter to him that there might be other ways of characterizing the same classes of sentences—ways that could be more illuminating for purposes other than his.

The two points are related, since there is no evident way of giving a general characterization of truth without introducing criteria

29

quite different in kind from those to which Tarski appealed. It is sometimes suggested by advocates of a deflationary view of truth that Convention-T provides an adequate answer to the question of what Tarski's various truth predicates have in common. But we should not be satisfied with this idea. For in those cases where the object language is contained in the metalanguage, the requirement is merely syntactical: it tells us something about the predicates, but not much about the concept. In other cases its application depends on our prior understanding of the notion of translation, a concept far more obscure than that of truth. The central point is this: aside from our grasp of the concept of translation, Convention-T gives us no idea how to tell in general when one of Tarski's truth predicates applies to a particular language. He does not define the concept of translation.[1]

We still lack, then, a satisfactory account of the general feature or features of the concept of truth which we cannot find in Tarski. Nevertheless, we can learn a great deal from Tarski. His constructions make it evident, for example, that, for a language with anything like the expressive power of a natural language, the class of true sentences cannot be characterized without introducing a relation like satisfaction, which connects words (singular terms, predicates) with objects. If we think of satisfaction as a generalized form of reference, Tarski has shown how the truth of sentences depends on the semantic features (e.g., reference) of certain proper parts of sentences. (Of course, Tarski no more defined the general concept of reference than he did that of truth.) Thus, even without an answer to the question of how we know when a definition of truth applies to a given language, Tarski has shown how the concept of

---

1. Michael Williams says a deflationist thinks that "what carries over from language to language . . . is the utility, for each language, of having its own disquotation device." Michael Williams, "Scepticism and Charity," *Ratio* (New Series), 1 (1988): 176–194; p. 180. But this is of no help in explaining how we can talk in one language about the truth of sentences in other languages.

truth can be used to give a clear description of a language. Of course, to give such a description, we must have a grasp of the concept of truth first; but we can have such a grasp without being able to formulate a systematic description of a language. Convention-T connects our untutored grasp of the concept with Tarski's ingenious machinery; it persuades us that the workings of the machinery pretty much accord with the concept as we know it.

This, then, is what we can learn about the concept of truth from Tarski; since it is obvious that he has not defined the general concept of truth, we can dismiss the suggestion that his stipulative definitions capture all there is to that concept. But there is no reason not to make use of the structure that went into Tarski's definitions. To do this, we do not need to make any change in Tarski's formal systems; once we realize that those systems do not reflect important aspects of the concepts of truth and reference, we can think of the truth and reference (satisfaction) predicates as primitives in the clauses that go into Tarski's recursive characterizations of reference and truth. If we find that the word 'definition' sorts ill with the idea that predicates are primitives, we can drop the word; this will not change the system. But to honor the recognition that the semantic predicates are primitives, we can drop the final step that for Tarski turns recursive characterizations into explicit definitions, and view the results as axiomatized theories of truth.[2]

2. Tarski recognized the possibility of giving axiomatic theories of truth, and remarked that "there is nothing essentially wrong in such an axiomatic procedure, and it may prove useful for various purposes." Alfred Tarski, "The Semantic Conception of Truth," *Philosophy and Phenomenological Research* 4 (1944): 341–376; p. 352. Tarski had a number of reasons for preferring an explicit definition to an axiomatic treatment of the concept of truth. First, he notes that the choice of axioms "has a rather accidental character, depending on inessential factors (such as e.g. the actual state of our knowledge)." Second, only an explicit definition can guarantee the consistency of the resulting system (given the consistency of the system prior to introducing the new primitive concepts); and, third, only an explicit definition can subdue doubts as to whether

An axiomatized theory of truth may be compared with, say, Kolmogorov's axiomatization of probability, which puts clear constraints on the concept of probability but leaves open such questions as whether probability is to be further characterized as relative frequency, degree of belief, or something else. Ramsey's axiomatic treatment of preference in the face of uncertainty, when applied to a particular agent, is analogous to an axiomatized theory of truth in the further respect that it yields a separate theory for each agent, just as Tarskian truth theories are peculiar to a language or, as I shall go on to propose, to an individual.

Just as a Tarskian theory does not tell us how to determine that the theory applies to a particular language or speaker, so nothing in Ramsey's theories tells us when such a theory applies to a particular agent. The issue in the case of decision theory is in part to specify the conditions an agent must satisfy in order to be said to prefer one object or course of action to another. In the case of a theory of truth, what we want to know is how to tell when T-sentences (and hence the theory as a whole) describe the language of a group or an individual. This obviously requires specifying at least part of the content of the concept of truth which Tarski's truth predicates fail to capture.

What do we add, then, to the properties of truth that Tarski has delineated when we apply the intuitive concept of truth? Aside from the view that Tarski said all that can or should be said about truth, a view that I discussed and rejected in the previous chapter, I think

the concept is "in harmony with the postulates of the unity of science and of physicalism." Alfred Tarski, "The Establishment of Scientific Semantics," in *Logic, Semantics, Metamathematics,* ed. J. H. Woodger (New York: Oxford University Press, 1956), pp. 401–408; pp. 405–406. The first danger is avoided if the axioms are restricted to the recursive clauses needed to characterize satisfaction; the second is (less conclusively) evaded as long as known ways of producing paradox are not introduced; and the threat that truth might not turn out to be reducible to physical concepts is a threat that, in my opinion, we neither can nor should want to escape.

most contemporary proposals fall into two broad categories: those which humanize truth by making it basically epistemic, and those which promote some form of correspondence theory.

Many philosophers, particularly recently, have held that truth is an epistemic concept; and even when they have not explicitly held this thesis, their views have often implied it. Coherence theories of truth are usually driven by an epistemic engine, as are pragmatic characterizations of truth. The antirealism of Dummett and Crispin Wright, Peirce's idea that the truth is where science will end up if it continues long enough, Richard Boyd's claim that truth is what explains the convergence of scientific theories, and Putnam's internal realism all include or entail an epistemic account of truth. Quine also, at least at times, has maintained that truth is internal to a theory of the world and so to that extent is dependent on our epistemological stance. Relativism about truth is perhaps always a symptom of infection by the epistemological virus; this seems to be true in any case for Quine, Nelson Goodman, and Putnam.

Apparently opposed to these views is the intuitive idea that truth, aside from a few special cases, is entirely independent of our beliefs; as it is sometimes put, our beliefs might be just as they are and yet reality—and so the truth about reality—be very different. According to this intuition, truth is "radically non-epistemic" (so Putnam characterizes "transcendental realism"), or "evidence-transcendent" (to use Dummett's phrase for realism). Both Putnam and Dummett are, of course, opposed to such views. If we were to look for tags for these two views of truth, we might hit on the adjectives 'epistemic' and 'realist'; the assertion of an essential tie to epistemology introduces a dependence of truth on what can somehow be verified by finite rational creatures, while the denial of any dependence of truth on belief or other human attitudes defines one philosophical use of the word 'realism.'

In the next chapter, I outline an approach to the concept of truth which rejects both of these views of truth. I do not aim to reconcile the two positions. I find epistemic views untenable, and realist views ultimately unintelligible. That both views, while no doubt answering to powerful intuitions, are fundamentally mistaken is at least suggested by the fact that both invite skepticism. Epistemic theories are skeptical in the way that idealism or phenomenalism is skeptical; they are skeptical not because they make reality unknowable, but because they reduce reality to so much less than we believe there is. Realist theories, on the other hand, seem to throw in doubt not only our knowledge of what is "evidence-transcendent," but all the rest of what we think we know, for such theories deny that what is true is conceptually connected in any way to what we believe.

Let us consider the project of giving content to a theory of truth. Tarski's definitions are normally reached through several steps. First, there is a definition of what it is to be a sentence in the object language; then there is a recursive characterization of a satisfaction relation (satisfaction is a highly generalized version of reference); the recursive characterization of satisfaction is turned into an explicit definition in the manner of Gottlob Frege and Dedekind; then truth is defined on the basis of the concepts of sentence and satisfaction. I am suggesting that we drop the last step that turns the recursive characterization of satisfaction into a definition, thus making explicit the fact that I am treating the truth and satisfaction predicates as primitives.

Which of the two semantic concepts, satisfaction or truth, we take as basic is, from a formal point of view, open to choice. Truth, as Tarski showed, is easily defined on the basis of satisfaction; but, alternatively, satisfaction can be taken to be whatever relation yields a correct account of truth. Tarski's work may seem to give uncertain signals. The fact that the truth of sentences is defined by appeal to the semantic properties of words suggests that, if we could give a satisfactory account of the semantic properties of words (essentially, of reference or satisfaction), we would understand the concept of truth. On the other hand, the key role of Convention-T in determining that truth, as characterized by the theory, has the same extension as the intuitive concept of truth makes it seem that it is truth rather than reference that is the basic primitive. The second is, I think, the right view. In his appeal to Convention-T, Tarski assumes, as we have seen, a prior grasp of the concept of truth; he then shows how this intuition can be implemented in detail for particular languages. The implementation requires the introduction of a referential concept, a relation between words and things, that is, some relation like satisfaction. The story about truth generates a pattern in language, the pattern of logical forms, or grammar properly conceived, and the network of semantic dependencies. There is no way to tell this story, which, being about truth, is about sentences or their occasions of use, without assigning semantical roles to the parts of sentences. But there is no appeal to a prior understanding of the concept of reference.

This way of viewing a theory of truth runs contrary to a tradition. According to the tradition, we could never come to understand sentences in their vast or even infinite array unless we understood the words drawn from a finite vocabulary which make them up; therefore, the semantic properties of words must be learned before we understand sentences, and the semantic properties of words have conceptual priority because it is they that explain the semantic properties—above all the truth conditions—of sentences. I think this line of argument, which starts with a truism, ends with a false conclusion; so something must have gone wrong. The mistake is to confuse the order of explanation that is appropriate once the theory is in place with the explanation of why the theory is correct. The theory is correct because it yields correct T-sentences; its correctness is tested against our grasp of the concept of truth as applied to sentences. Since T-sentences say nothing whatever about reference, satisfaction, or expressions that are not sentences, the test of the correctness of the theory is independent of intuitions concerning these concepts. Once we have the theory, though, we can explain the truth of sentences on the basis of their structure and the semantic properties of the parts. The analogy with theories in science is complete: in order to organize and explain what we directly observe, we posit unobserved or indirectly observed objects and forces; the theory is tested by what is directly observed.

The perspective on language and truth that we have gained is this: what is open to observation is the use of sentences in context, and truth is the semantic concept we understand best. Reference and related semantic notions like satisfaction are, by comparison, theoretical concepts (as are the notions of singular term, predicate, sentential connective, and the rest). There can be no question about the correctness of these theoretical concepts beyond the question whether they yield a satisfactory account of the use of sentences.

One effect of these reflections is to focus on the centrality of the concept of truth in the understanding of language; it is our grasp of this concept that permits us to make sense of the question whether a theory of truth for a language is correct. There is no reason to look for a prior, or independent, account of some referential relation. The other main consequence of the present stance is that it provides an opportunity to say fairly sharply what is missing, as an account of truth, in a theory of truth in Tarski's style.

What is missing is the connection with the users of language. Nothing would count as a sentence, and the concept of truth would have no application, if there were not creatures who used sentences by uttering or inscribing tokens of them. Any complete account of the concept of truth must relate it to actual linguistic intercourse. Put more precisely: the question whether a theory of truth is true of a given language (that is, of a speaker or group of speakers) makes sense only if the sentences of that language have a meaning that is independent of the theory (otherwise the theory is not a theory in the ordinary sense, but a description of a possible language). Or to return to the definitional form that Tarski favored: if the question can be raised whether a truth definition really does define truth for a given language, the language must have a life independent of the definition (otherwise the definition is merely stipulative: it specifies, but is not true of, a language).

If we knew in general what makes a theory of truth correctly apply to a speaker or group of speakers, we could plausibly be said to understand the concept of truth; and if we could say exactly what makes such a theory true, we could give an explicit account—perhaps a definition—of truth. The ultimate evidence, as opposed to a criterion, for the correctness of a theory of truth for a language must lie in available facts about how speakers use the language. When I say available, I mean publicly available—available not only in principle, but available in practice to anyone who is capable of understanding the speaker or speakers of the language. Since all of us do understand some speakers of some languages, all of us must have adequate evidence for attributing truth conditions to the utterances of some speakers; all of us have, therefore, a competent grasp of the concept of truth as applied to the speech behavior of others.

Have we now settled the question whether truth is radically non-epistemic, as realists aver, or basically epistemic, as others maintain? It may seem that the matter has been settled in favor of the epistemic or subjective view, since we have followed a course of argument that leads to the conclusion that it is how language is used which decides whether a theory of truth for that language is true. But in fact the matter is not settled, for it may be held by realists that the question whether the theory is true for a given language or group of speakers is indeed empirical, but only because the question of what the words mean is empirical; the issue of truth, it may be held, remains to be answered, whether by the theory itself or in some other way.

Does the theory already contain the answer? It does if there is substance to the claim that a Tarski-type theory of truth is a correspondence theory, for then the theory must in effect define truth to be correspondence with reality; this is the classical form of realism with respect to truth. Tarski himself said he wanted his truth definitions to "do justice to the intuitions which adhere to the *classical conception of truth*"; he then quotes Aristotle's *Metaphysics* ("to say of what is that it is, or of what is not that it is not, is true"), and offers as an alternative formulation,

> *The truth of a sentence consists in its agreement with (or correspondence to) reality.*

(Tarski adds that the term 'correspondence theory' has been suggested for this way of putting things.)[3] I have myself argued in the past that theories of the sort that Tarski showed how to produce were correspondence theories of a sort.[4] I said this on the ground that there is no way to give such a theory without employing a concept like reference or satisfaction which relates expressions to objects in the world.

It was a mistake to call such theories correspondence theories. The usual complaint about correspondence theories is that it makes no sense to suggest that it is somehow possible to compare one's words or beliefs with the world, since the attempt must always end up simply with the acquisition of more beliefs. This complaint was voiced, for example, by Otto Neurath, who for this reason adopted a coherence view of truth;[5] Carl Hempel expressed the

3. Tarski, "The Semantic Conception of Truth," pp. 342–343. Tarski also speaks of sentences "describing . . . states of affairs"; ibid., p. 345. Cf. Tarski, "The Concept of Truth in Formalized Languages," in *Logic, Semantics, Metamathematics*, ed. Woodger, pp. 152–278, p. 153; and Tarski, "The Establishment of Scientific Semantics," p. 403.

4. In Donald Davidson, "True to the Facts," *Inquiries into Truth and Interpretation*, 2nd ed. (New York: Oxford, 2001). The argument is this. Truth is defined on the basis of satisfaction: a sentence of the object language is true if and only if it is satisfied by every sequence of the objects over which the variables of quantification of the object language range. Take "corresponds to" as "satisfies," and you have defined truth as correspondence. The oddity of the idea is evident from the counterintuitive and contrived nature of the entities to which sentences "correspond," and from the fact that all true sentences would correspond to the same entity.

5. Otto Neurath, "Protokollsätze," *Erkenntnis* 3 (1932/33): 204–214.

same objection, speaking of the "fatal confrontation of statements and facts."[6] Rorty has insisted, claiming sympathy with Dewey, that a correspondence view of truth makes the concept of truth useless.[7]

This complaint against correspondence theories is not sound. One reason it is not sound is that it depends on assuming that some form of epistemic theory is correct; therefore, it would be a legitimate complaint only if truth were an epistemic concept. For why would one object to a correspondence theory as making truth "useless" or senseless unless he or she thought a useful theory would make truth epistemically accessible? If this were the only reason for rejecting correspondence theories, the realist could simply reply that his position is untouched—he always maintained that truth was independent of our beliefs or our ability to learn the truth.

The real objection to correspondence theories is simpler: it is that there is nothing interesting or instructive to which true sentences correspond. The point was made some time ago by C. I. Lewis;[8] he challenged the correspondence theorist to locate the fact or part of reality, or of the world, to which a true sentence corresponded. One can locate individual objects, if the sentence happens to name or de-

6. Carl Hempel, "On the Logical Positivist's Theory of Truth," *Analysis* 2 (1935): 49–59; p. 51.

7. Richard Rorty, *Consequences of Pragmatism* (Minneapolis: University of Minnesota Press, 1982), Introduction; see also Rorty, "Pragmatism, Davidson, and Truth," in *Truth and Interpretation*, ed. E. Lepore (New York: Blackwell, 1986), pp. 333–355. I was persuaded by Rorty not to call my position either a correspondence theory or a coherence theory; I may have persuaded him to give up the pragmatist theory of truth. See Rorty, "Pragmatism, Davidson, and Truth."

For an example of the use of 'correspondence' I now deplore, see my "A Coherence Theory of Truth and Knowledge," in *Subjective, Intersubjective, Objective* (New York: Oxford, 2001), pp. 137–153, and "Afterthoughts," in *Subjective, Intersubjective, Objective*, pp. 154–158.

8. C. I. Lewis, *An Analysis of Knowledge and Valuation* (La Salle, Ill.: Open Court, 1946), pp. 50–55.

scribe them, but even such location makes sense relative only to a frame of reference, and so presumably the frame of reference must be included in whatever it is to which a true sentence corresponds. Following out this line of thought led Lewis to conclude that, if true sentences correspond to anything at all, it must be the universe as a whole; thus, all true sentences correspond to the same thing. Frege, as we know, reached the same conclusion through a somewhat similar course of reasoning. Frege's argument, if Alonzo Church is right,[9] can be formalized: starting from the assumptions that a true sentence cannot be made to correspond to something different by the substitution of co-referring singular terms, or by the substitution of logically equivalent sentences, it is easy to show that, if true sentences correspond to anything, they all correspond to the same thing. But this is to trivialize the concept of correspondence completely; there is no interest in the relation of correspondence if there is only one thing to which to correspond, since, as in any such case, the relation may as well be collapsed into a simple property: thus, "*s* corresponds to the universe," like "*s* corresponds to (or names) the True" or "*s* corresponds to the facts," can less misleadingly be read "*s* is true." Peter Strawson has observed that the parts of a sentence may correspond to parts of the world (that is, refer to them), but adds:

> It is evident that there is nothing else in the world for the statement itself to be related to. . . . And it is evident that the demand that there should be such a relatum is logically absurd. . . . But the demand for something in the world *which makes the statement true . . ., or to which the statement corresponds when it is true,* is just this demand.[10]

9. The argument, attributed to Frege by Church, can be found in Church's *Introduction to Mathematical Logic*, vol. 1 (Princeton: Princeton University Press, 1956), pp. 24–25. For further discussion of this argument, see Chapter 6.

10. Peter Strawson, "Truth," *Proceedings of the Aristotelian Society,* Supplementary Volume 24 (1950): 129–156; pp. 194–195 of reprint in Strawson, *Logico-Linguistic Papers* (London: Methuen, 1971).

He correctly goes on to claim that, "while we certainly say that a statement corresponds to (fits, is borne out by, agrees with) the facts," this is merely "a variant on saying it is true."

The correct objection to correspondence theories is not, then, that they make truth something to which humans can never legitimately aspire; the real objection is rather that such theories fail to provide entities to which truth vehicles (whether we take these to be statements, sentences, or utterances) can be said to correspond. If this is right, and I am convinced it is, we ought also to question the popular assumption that sentences, or their spoken tokens, or sentence-like entities or configurations in our brains, can properly be called "representations," since there is nothing for them to represent. If we give up facts as entities that make sentences true, we ought to give up representations at the same time, for the legitimacy of each depends on the legitimacy of the other.

There is thus a serious reason to regret having said that a Tarski-style truth theory was a form of correspondence theory. My basic reason for saying it was not was that I had made the mistake of supposing sentences or utterances of sentences corresponded to anything in an interesting way. But I was still under the influence of the idea that there is something important in the realist conception of truth—the idea that truth, and therefore reality, are (except for special cases) independent of what anyone believes or can know. Thus, I advertised my view as a brand of realism, realism with respect to the "external world," with respect to meaning, and with respect to truth.[11]

The terms 'realism' and 'correspondence' were ill-chosen because they suggest the positive endorsement of a position, or an assumption that there is a clear positive thesis to be adopted, whereas all I was entitled to maintain, and all that my position actually entailed with respect to realism and truth, was the negative view that epistemic views are false. The realist view of truth, if it has any con-

11. Davidson, "A Coherence Theory of Truth and Knowledge," p. 307.

tent, must be based on the idea of correspondence, correspondence as applied to sentences or beliefs or utterances—entities that are propositional in character; and such correspondence cannot be made intelligible. I made the mistake of assuming that realism and epistemic theories exhausted the possible positions. The only legitimate reason I had for calling my position a form of realism was to reject positions like Dummett's antirealism; I was concerned to reject the doctrine that either reality or truth depends directly on our epistemic powers. There is a point in such a rejection. But it is futile either to reject or to accept the slogan that the real and the true are "independent of our beliefs." The only evident positive sense we can make of this phrase, the only use that consorts with the intentions of those who prize it, derives from the idea of correspondence, and this is an idea without content.[12]

To reject the doctrine that the real and true are independent of our beliefs is not, of course, to reject the platitude it can mistakenly be thought to express: believing something does not in general make it true. For allowing that the platitude is true does not commit us to saying there is no connection whatever between belief and truth; there must be some connection if we are to relate the truth of utterances to their use. The question is what that connection can be.

Various forms of subjectivism—that is, of views that make truth out to be an epistemic concept—connect human thoughts, desires, and intentions to truth in quite different ways, and I cannot pretend to do justice to all such views here. The best I can do is indicate why, despite the differences among the various positions, it makes sense to be dissatisfied with them all.

I have classified coherence theories of truth as epistemic, and this

12. Arthur Fine gives up on realism for some of the same reasons I do, and he adds a splendid refutation of the thesis that a realistic view of truth explains the practice and advance of science. See "The Natural Ontological Attitude," in *The Shaky Game: Einstein, Realism, and the Quantum Theory,* 2nd ed. (Chicago: University of Chicago Press, 1986), pp. 112–135.

needs an explanation. A pure coherence theory of truth would hold, I suppose, that all the sentences in a consistent set of sentences are true. Perhaps no one has ever held such a theory, for it is mad. Those who have proposed coherence theories, for example Neurath and Rudolf Carnap (at one time), have usually made clear that it was sets of *beliefs,* or of sentences held to be true, whose consistency was enough to make them true. This is why I class coherence theories with epistemic views: they tie truth directly to what is believed. But unless something further is added, this view seems as wrong as Moritz Schlick held it to be (he called it an "astounding error");[13] the obvious objection is that many different consistent sets of beliefs are possible which are not consistent with one another.[14]

There are theories, similar in certain ways to coherence theories, which have much the same drawback. Quine holds that the truth of some sentences, which he calls observation sentences, is tied directly to experience; further sentences derive their empirical content from their connections with observation sentences and their logical relations to one another. The truth of the resulting theory depends only on how well it serves to explain or predict true observation sentences. Quine plausibly maintains that there could be two theories equally capable of accounting for all true observation sentences, and yet such that neither theory can be reduced to the other (each theory contains at least one predicate that cannot be defined using the resources of the other theory). Quine has at different

13. Moritz Schlick, "Über das Fundament der Erkenntnis," *Erkenntnis* 4 (1934): 79–99.

14. Not every theory that relates truth to coherent sets of beliefs is wrong. What must be added to standard coherence theories is an appreciation not only of how beliefs are causally and logically related to each other, but of how the contents of a belief depends on its causal connections with the world. I discuss these matters in the next chapter. See also my "A Coherence Theory of Truth and Knowledge," and "Empirical Content" in *Subjective, Intersubjective, Objective,* pp. 159–176.

times embraced different ways of thinking of this situation. According to one way, both theories are true. I see no reason to object to the view that empirically equivalent theories (however one characterizes empirical content) are true or false together. According to Quine's other view, a speaker or thinker at a given time operates with one theory and, for him at that time, the theory he is using is true and the other theory false. If he shifts to the alternative theory, then *it* becomes true and the previously accepted theory false. The position may illustrate what Quine means when he says that truth is "immanent."[15] This conception of the immanence or relativity of truth should not be confused with the pedestrian sense in which the truth of sentences is relative to the language in which they occur. Quine's two theories can belong to, and be stated in, the same language; indeed, they must be if we are to understand the claim that the theories conflict. It is not easy to see how the same sentence (without indexical elements), with interpretation unchanged, can be true for one person and not for another, or for a given person at one time and not at another. The difficulty seems to result from the attempt to import epistemological considerations into the concept of truth.[16]

Putnam's "internal realism" also makes truth immanent, though not, as Quine's view does, relative to a theory, but to the entire language and conceptual scheme a person accepts. Of course, if all this

15. See W. V. Quine, *Ontological Relativity and Other Essays* (New York: Columbia University Press, 1969). For Quine's problem about empirically equivalent, mutually irreducible theories, see his "On Empirically Equivalent Systems of the World," *Erkenntnis* 9 (1975): 313–328; *Theories and Things* (Cambridge, Mass.: Harvard University Press, 1981), pp. 29–30; and "Reply to Roger F. Gibson Jr.," in *The Philosophy of W. V. Quine,* ed. L. E. Hahn and P. A. Schilpp (Lasalle, Ill.: Open Court, 1986), pp. 155–158; pp. 156–157.

16. Quine may not have intended the "immanence" of truth to have meant any more than that the truth of sentences (or utterances) is relative to a language. See my "What Is Quine's View of Truth?" *Inquiry* 37 (1994): 437–440, and Quine's reply, "Responses," *Inquiry* 37 (1994): 495–505.

means is that the truth of sentences or utterances is relative to a language, that is familiar and trivially correct. But Putnam seems to have something more in mind—for example, that a sentence of yours and a sentence of mine may contradict each other, and yet each be true "for the speaker." It is hard to think in what language this position can be coherently expressed. The source of the trouble is once again the felt need to make truth accessible. Putnam is clear that this is the consideration that concerns him. He identifies truth explicitly with idealized justified assertability. He calls this a form of realism because there is "a fact of the matter as to what the verdict would be if the conditions were sufficiently good, a verdict to which opinion would 'converge' if we were reasonable."[17] He adds that his view is "a *human* kind of realism, a belief that there is a fact of the matter as to what is rightly assertable for us, as opposed to what is rightly assertable from the God's eye view so dear to the classical metaphysical realist." One suspects that, if the conditions under which someone is ideally justified in asserting something were spelled out, it would be apparent either that those conditions allow the possibility of error or that they are so ideal as to make no use of the intended connection with human abilities. It is also striking that Putnam seems to have no argument for his position except that the alternative, "metaphysical realism," is unacceptable. He does not argue that there can be no other position.

Putnam describes his position as close to Dummett's on the main point—the epistemological status of truth. One difference is that Putnam is less certain than Dummett that truth is limited to what is definitely ascertainable, and therefore he is less sure that the principle of bivalence must be abandoned; this perhaps explains why Putnam calls his view a form of realism while Dummett calls his position antirealist. Putnam also thinks he differs from Dummett in

17. Hilary Putnam, *Realism and Reason: Philosophical Papers*, vol. 3 (New York: Cambridge University Press, 1983), p. xviii.

tying truth to *idealized* justified assertability instead of justified assertability; but here I think a close reading of Dummett would show that he has much the same idea. If Dummett does not insist on something similar to Putnam's ideal conditions, then I think a criticism of Dummett that Putnam once formulated applies: if truth depends simply on justified assertability, truth can be "lost," that is, a sentence can be true for a person at a particular time and later become false because the conditions of justification change. This must be wrong.[18] Dummett says he agrees that truth cannot be lost, but he fails to give a clear idea of how warranted assertability can be both a fixed property *and* a property that depends on the actual ability of human speakers to recognize that certain conditions are satisfied. Actual abilities wax and wane, and differ from person to person; truth does not.

Why does Dummett endorse this view of truth? There are a number of reasons, but one seems to be this. We have seen that a theory of truth in Tarski's style neither defines nor fully characterizes truth; there is no way to tell if the theory applies to a speaker or group of speakers unless something is added to relate the theory to the human uses of language. Dummett thinks the only way to do this is to make truth humanly recognizable. The human use of language must be a function of how people understand the language, so if truth is to play a role in explaining what it is to understand a language, there must be something, Dummett thinks, that counts as a person having "conclusive evidence" that a statement is true. One can appreciate the force of this idea while finding it difficult to accept. I have given my chief reason for rejecting it—that it is either empty, or it makes truth a property that can be lost. But it is important to realize that there are other strong intuitions that would also

18. Hilary Putnam, "Reference and Understanding," in *Meaning and Use,* ed. A. Margalit (Dordrecht: Reidel, 1979), and "Reply to Dummett's Comment," in *Meaning and Use,* ed. A. Margalit (Dordrecht: Reidel, 1979), pp. 226–228.

have to be sacrificed if Dummett were right. One is the connection of truth with meaning: on Dummett's view, we can understand a sentence like 'A city will never be built on this spot' without having any idea what it would be for this sentence to be true (since the sentence, or an utterance of it, has no truth value for Dummett). Another is the connection of truth with belief: on Dummett's view, I can understand and believe a city will never be built on this spot, but my belief will have no truth value. It would seem that, for Dummett, having a belief that one expresses by a sentence one understands is not necessarily to believe that the sentence is true.

I might be tempted to go along with Dummett if I thought we must choose between what Putnam calls transcendental realism, i.e., the view that truth is "radically non-epistemic," that all of our best researched and established beliefs and theories may be false, and Dummett's identification of truth with warranted assertability, since I find the former view—essentially the correspondence view—incomprehensible, while I find Dummett's view merely false. But I see no reason to suppose that realism and antirealism, explained in terms of the radically nonepistemic or the radically epistemic character of truth, are the only ways to give substance to a theory of truth or meaning.

Let us briefly take stock. In the first chapter, I rejected deflationary views of truth, those which teach that there is no more to the concept than Tarski has shown how to define for particular languages. In the present chapter, I have argued that certain familiar attempts to characterize truth which go beyond giving empirical content to a structure of the sort Tarski taught us how to describe are empty, false, or confused. We should not say that truth is correspondence, coherence, warranted assertability, ideally justified assertability, what is accepted in the conversation of the right people, what science will end up maintaining, what explains the convergence on final theories in science, or the success of our ordinary beliefs. To the extent that realism and antirealism depend on one or another of these views of truth, we should refuse to endorse either. Realism, with its insistence on radically nonepistemic correspondence, asks more of truth than we can understand; antirealism, with its limitation of truth to what can be ascertained, deprives truth of its role as an intersubjective standard. We must find another way of viewing the matter.

CHAPTER 3

The Content of the Concept of Truth

A *theory* of truth, in contrast to a stipulative *definition* of truth, is an empirical theory about the truth conditions of every sentence in some corpus of sentences. But of course sentences are abstract objects, shapes, say, and do not have truth conditions except as embodied in sounds and scribbles by speakers and scribblers. In the end, it is the utterances and writings of language users with which a theory of truth must deal; the role of sentences in a theory is merely to make it possible to deal with types of utterances and inscriptions, whether or not particular types are realized. Introducing sentences thus serves two purposes: it allows us to speak of all actual utterances and inscriptions of the same type in one breath; and it allows us to stipulate what the truth conditions of an utterance or inscription of a given type would be if it were uttered. (For brevity, I shall from here on refer to acts of writing as utterances along with their audible counterparts.)

Although we may sometimes say that a group speaks with one voice, utterances are essentially personal; each utterance has its agent and its time. An utterance is an event of a special sort, an intentional action. Theories of truth are primarily concerned with sentential utterances, utterances which, whatever their surface grammar may be, must be treated as utterances of sentences. The primacy of sentences or sentential utterances is dictated by the fact that it is sentences, as uttered on particular occasions by particular speakers, for which the theory supplies truth conditions and of which truth is predicated. Verbal felicity apart, there is no reason not to call the utterance of a sentence, under conditions that make the sentence true, a true utterance.

A theory of truth does more than describe an aspect of the speech behavior of an agent, for it not only gives the truth conditions of the actual utterances of the agent; it also specifies the conditions under which the utterance of a sentence would be true if it were uttered. This applies both to sentences actually uttered, by telling us what would have been the case if those sentences had been uttered at other times or under other circumstances, and to sentences never uttered. The theory thus describes a certain complex ability.

An utterance has certain truth conditions only if the speaker intends it to be interpreted as having those truth conditions. Moral, social, or legal considerations may sometimes invite us to deny this, but I do not think the reasons for such exceptions reveal anything of importance about what is basic to communication. Someone may say something that would normally be offensive or insulting in a language he believes his hearers do not understand; but in this case his audience for the purpose of interpretation is obviously just the speaker himself. A malapropism or slip of the tongue, if it means anything, means what its promulgator intends it to mean. There are those who are pleased to hold that the meanings of words are magically independent of the speaker's intentions—for example, that they depend on how the majority, or the best-informed, or the best-born, of the community in which the speaker lives speak, or perhaps how they would speak if they took enough care.[1] This

1. Saul Kripke attributes such a view to Wittgenstein in *Wittgenstein on Rules and Private Language* (Cambridge, Mass.: Harvard University Press, 1982), and tentatively endorses it. For a different version, see the numerous works of Tyler Burge on anti-individualism, e.g., "Individualism and the Mental," *Midwest Studies in Philosophy* 4 (1979): 73–121; "Individualism and Psy-

doctrine entails that a speaker may be perfectly intelligible to his hearers, may be interpreted exactly as he intends to be interpreted, and yet may not know what he means by what he says. I think that this view, although it has been elaborately and ingeniously defended, reveals nothing of serious philosophical interest about the nature of truth or meaning (though it may have much to do with good, or acceptable, manners, and may represent an intention, or even some sort of social responsibility, on the part of some speakers).[2] For the purpose of the present enterprise, that of understanding truth and meaning, we should, I think, stick as closely as possible to what is made directly available to an audience by a speaker, and this is the relevant state of the speaker's mind. What matters to successful linguistic communication is the intention of the speaker to be interpreted in a certain way, on the one hand, and the actual interpretation of the speaker's words along the intended lines through the interpreter's recognition of the speaker's intentions, on the other.[3]

The approach I am following puts no primary weight on the concept of a language as something shared by a speaker and an inter-

chology," *The Philosophical Review* 95 (1986): 3–45; and "Wherein Is Language Social?" in *Reflections on Chomsky*, ed. Alexander George (London: Basil Blackwell, 1989), pp. 176–191.

2. See my "Knowing One's Own Mind," *Subjective, Intersubjective, Objective* (New York: Oxford University Press, 2001), pp. 15–38.

3. The influence of H. P. Grice's "Meaning," *The Philosophical Review* 66 (1957): 377–388, will be evident here. My characterization of successful communication leaves open a range of possibilities with respect to the question of what a speaker means by her words on occasion. Since the speaker must intend to be interpreted in a certain way, she must believe that her audience is equipped to interpret her words in that way. But how well justified must this belief be, and how nearly correct? I do not believe our standards for deciding what someone's words, as spoken on a given occasion, mean are firm enough to let us draw a sharp line between a failed intention that one's words have a certain meaning and a success at meaning accompanied by a failed intention to be interpreted as intended.

preter, or by a speaker and a speech community, except in this sense: although communication by speech does not, as far as I can see, require that any two speakers *speak* in the same way, it does, of course, demand a fit between how speakers intend to be interpreted and how their interpreters understand them. This demand no doubt tends to encourage convergence in speech behavior among those who exchange words, the degree depending on factors like shared social and economic status, educational and ethnic background, and so on. What convergence exists is of such vast practical importance that we may exaggerate both its degree and its philosophical significance. But I think we do well to ignore this practical issue in constructing theories of meaning, of truth, and of linguistic communication.[4] I shall therefore treat theories of truth as applicable in the first place to individual speakers at various periods or even moments of their lives.

A theory of truth links speaker with interpreter: it at once describes the linguistic abilities and practices of the speaker and gives the substance of what a knowledgeable interpreter knows which enables him to grasp the meaning of the speaker's utterances. This is not to say that either speaker or interpreter is aware of or has propositional knowledge of the contents of such a theory. The theory describes the conditions under which an utterance of a speaker is true, and so says nothing directly about what the speaker knows. The theory does, however, imply something about the propositional content of certain intentions of the speaker, namely, the intentions that his utterances be interpreted in a certain way. And though the interpreter certainly does not need to have explicit knowledge of the theory, the theory does provide the only way to specify the infinity of things the interpreter knows about the speaker, namely, the conditions under which each of an indefinitely large number of sentences of the speaker would be true if uttered.

4. See my "Communication and Convention," *Inquiries into Truth and Interpretation*, 2nd ed. (New York: Oxford University Press, 2001), pp. 265–280.

There must, of course, be *some* sense in which speaker and interpreter have internalized a theory; but this comes to no more than the fact that the speaker is able to speak as if he believed the interpreter would interpret him in the way the theory describes, and the fact that the interpreter is prepared to interpret him in this way. All we should require of a theory of truth for a speaker is that it be such that, if an interpreter had explicit propositional knowledge of the theory, he would know the truth conditions of the utterances of the speaker.[5]

A theory of truth for a speaker is a theory of meaning in this sense, that explicit knowledge of the theory would suffice for understanding the utterances of that speaker. It accomplishes this by describing the critical core of the speaker's potential and actual linguistic behavior—in effect, how the speaker intends his utterances to be interpreted. The sort of understanding involved is restricted to what we may as well call the literal meaning of the words, by which I mean, roughly, the meaning the speaker intends the interpreter to grasp, whatever further force or significance the speaker may want the interpreter to fathom.[6]

5. This is, of course, far more than is provided by any theory anyone has been able to provide for any natural language. The condition is therefore not one we know could be satisfied. We do, on the other hand, know how to produce such a theory for a powerful, perhaps self-sufficient, fragment of English and other natural languages, and this is enough to give substance to the idea that the incorporation of the concept of truth in a theory provides insight into the nature of the concept. We may in the end have to settle for a far looser sense of "theory" than Tarski had in mind. I am skipping a host of well-exercised problems, such as providing truth conditions for subjunctive conditionals, imperatives, interrogatives, ethical statements, etc. I have discussed (though certainly not solved) most of these problems elsewhere.

6. There is one intention not touched on by a theory of truth which a speaker must intend an interpreter to perceive: the force of the utterance. An interpreter must, if he is to understand a speaker, be able to tell whether an utterance is intended as a joke, an assertion, an order, a question, and so forth. I do not believe there are rules or conventions that govern this essential aspect of lan-

The thesis that a theory of truth conditions gives an adequate account of what is needed for understanding the literal meanings of utterances is, of course, much disputed, but since I have argued for it at length elsewhere, I will for the most part treat the thesis here as an assumption. If the assumption is mistaken, much of the detail in what I shall go on to say about the application of the concept of truth will be threatened, but the general approach will, I think, remain valid.

A theory of truth, viewed as an empirical theory, is tested by its relevant consequences, and these are the T-sentences entailed by the theory. A T-sentence says of a particular speaker that, every time he utters a given sentence, the utterance will be true if and only if certain conditions are satisfied. T-sentences thus have the form and function of natural laws; they are universally quantified bi-conditionals, and as such are understood to apply counterfactually and to be confirmed by their instances.[7] Thus, a theory of truth is a theory for describing, explaining, understanding, and predicting a basic aspect of verbal behavior. Since the concept of truth is central to the theory, we are justified in saying that truth is a crucially important explanatory concept.

The question that remains is: How do we confirm the truth of a

guage. It is something that language users can convey to hearers and hearers can, often enough, detect; but this does not show that these abilities can be regimented. I believe there are sound reasons for thinking that nothing like a serious theory is possible concerning this dimension of language. Still less are there conventions or rules for creating or understanding metaphors, irony, humor, etc. See my "What Metaphors Mean," *Inquiries into Truth and Interpretation,* 2nd ed. (New York: Oxford University Press, 2001), pp. 245–264, and "Communication and Convention."

7. This goes some way toward answering a frequent criticism of theories of truth as theories of meaning. For example, given the (unusual) case of two unstructured predicates with the same extension, a theory of truth may make a distinction if there are circumstances which never arise but under which the truth conditions would be different.

T-sentence? This is a kind of question that arises with respect to many theories, both in the physical sciences and in psychology. A theory of fundamental measurement of weight, for example, states in axiomatic form the properties of the relation between x and y that holds when x is at least as heavy as y; this relation must, among other things, be transitive, reflexive, and nonsymmetric. A theory of preference may stipulate that the relation of weak preference has the same formal properties. But in neither case do the axioms define the central relation (x is at least as heavy as y, x is weakly preferred to y), nor do they instruct us how to determine when the relation holds. Before the theory can be tested or used, something must be said about the interpretation of the undefined concepts. The same applies to the concept of truth.[8]

It is a mistake to look for an explicit definition or outright reduction of the concept of truth. Truth is one of the clearest and most basic concepts we have, so it is fruitless to dream of eliminating it in favor of something simpler or more fundamental. Our procedure is rather this: we have asked what the formal properties of the concept are when it is applied to relatively well-understood structures, namely, languages. Here Tarski's work provides the inspiration. It remains to indicate how a theory of truth can be applied to particular speakers or groups of speakers. Given the complexity of the structures the concept of truth helps characterize, comparatively anemic bits of evidence, applied at a potential infinity of points, can yield rich and instructive results. But complete formalization of the relation between evidence for the theory and the theory itself is not to be expected.

What we *should* demand, however, is that the evidence for the

8. I explained in the last chapter why I believe we do not need to worry separately about reference or satisfaction. Put briefly, the reason is that T-sentences do not contain a referential concept. Since the testable implications of the theory are T-sentences as applied to cases, any way of characterizing satisfaction that yields confirmable T-sentences is as good as another.

theory be in principle publicly accessible, and that it not assume in advance the concepts to be illuminated. The requirement that the evidence be publicly accessible is not due to an atavistic yearning for behavioristic or verificationist foundations, but to the fact that what is to be explained is a social phenomenon. Mental phenomena in general may or may not be private, but the correct interpretation of one person's speech by another must *in principle* be possible. A speaker's intention that her words be understood in a certain way may of course remain opaque to even the most skilled and knowledgeable listener, but what has to do with correct interpretation, meaning, and truth conditions is necessarily based on available evidence. As Wittgenstein has insisted, not to mention Dewey, G. H. Mead, Quine, and many others, language is intrinsically social. This does not entail that truth and meaning can be *defined* in terms of observable behavior, or that they are "nothing but" observable behavior; but it does imply that meaning is entirely determined by observable behavior, even readily observable behavior. That meanings are decipherable is not a matter of luck; public availability is a constitutive aspect of language.

The concepts used to express the evidence must not beg the question; they should be sufficiently remote from what the theory ultimately produces. This final condition is no more than we ask of any revealing analysis, but it is difficult, at least in this case, to satisfy it. Any attempt to understand verbal communication must view it in its natural setting as part of a larger enterprise. It seems at first that this cannot be difficult, there being no more to language than public transactions among speakers and interpreters, and the aptitudes for such transactions. Yet the task eludes us. For the fact that linguistic phenomena are nothing but behavioral, biological, or physical phenomena described in an exotic vocabulary of meaning, reference, truth, assertion, and so on—mere supervenience of this sort of one kind of fact or description on another—does not guarantee, or even hold out promise of, the possibility of conceptual reduction.

Therein lies our problem. I shall now sketch what I think is the right *sort* of solution. The immediate psychological environment of linguistic aptitudes and accomplishments is to be found in the attitudes, states, and events that are described in intensional idiom: intentional action, desires, beliefs, and their close relatives like hopes, fears, wishes, and attempts. Not only do the various propositional attitudes and their conceptual attendants form the setting in which speech occurs, but there is no chance of arriving at a deep understanding of linguistic facts except as that understanding is accompanied by an interlocking account of the central cognitive and conative attitudes.

It is too much to ask that these basic intensional notions be reduced to something else—something more behavioristic, neurological, or physiological, for example. Nor can we analyze any of these basic three—belief, desire, and meaning—in terms of one or two of the others; or so I think, and have argued elsewhere.[9] But even if we could effect a reduction in this basic trio, the results would fall short of what might be wanted simply because the end point—the interpretation, say, of speech—would lie too close to where we began (with belief and desire, or with intention, which is the product of belief and desire). A basic account of any of these concepts must start beyond or beneath them all, or at some point equidistant from them all.

If this is so, an analysis of linguistic meaning that assumes prior identification of nonlinguistic purposes or intentions will be radically incomplete. Nor will it help to appeal to explicit or implicit rules or conventions, if only because these must be understood in

9. For considerations in support of these claims, see my "Radical Interpretation," "Belief and the Basis of Meaning," and "Thought and Talk," Essays 9, 10, and 11, in *Inquiries into Truth and Interpretation,* 2nd ed. (New York: Oxford University Press, 2001), pp. 125–140, 141–154, and 155–170, respectively, and "Three Varieties of Knowledge," Essay 14, in *Subjective, Intersubjective, Objective* (New York: Oxford University Press, 2001), pp. 15–38.

terms of intentions and beliefs. Conventions and rules do not explain language; language explains them. There is no doubting, of course, the importance of showing how meanings and intentions are connected. Such connections give structure to the propositional attitudes and suit them to systematic treatment. But the interdependence of the basic intentional attitudes is so complete that it is bootless to hope to understand one independently of understanding the others. What is wanted, then, is an approach that yields an interpretation of a speaker's words at the same time that it provides a basis for attributing beliefs and desires to the speaker. Such an approach aims to provide a basis for, rather than to assume, the individuation of propositional attitudes.

Bayesian decision theory, as developed by Frank Ramsey,[10] deals with two of the three intentional aspects of rationality that seem most fundamental, belief and desire. The choice of one course of action over another, or the preference that one state of affairs obtain rather than another, is the product of two considerations: the value placed on the various possible consequences, and how likely those consequences are deemed to be, given that the action is performed or the state of affairs comes to obtain. In choosing an action or state of affairs, therefore, a rational agent will select one, the relative value of whose possible outcomes, when tempered by the probability the agent assigns to those consequences, is greatest. Acting is always a gamble, since an agent can never be certain how things will turn out. So to the extent that an agent is rational, he will take what he believes is the best bet available (he "maximizes expected utility").

A feature of such a theory is that what it is designed to explain—ordinal preferences or choices among options—is relatively open to observation, while the explanatory mechanism, which involves de-

10. F. P. Ramsey, "Truth and Probability," in *Philosophical Papers*, ed. D. H. Mellor (Cambridge: Cambridge University Press, 1990).

gree of belief and cardinal values, is not taken to be observable. The issue therefore arises of how to tell when a person has a certain degree of belief in some proposition, or what the relative strengths of his preferences are. The evident problem is that what is known (ordinal, or simple preference) is the resultant of two unknowns, degree of belief and relative strength of preference. If a person's cardinal preferences for outcomes were known, then his choices among courses of action would reveal his degree of belief; and if his degree of belief were known, his choices would disclose the comparative values he puts on the outcomes. But how can both unknowns be determined from simple choices or preference alone? Ramsey solved this problem by showing how, on the basis of simple choices alone, it is possible to find a proposition treated as being as likely to be true as its negation. This single proposition can then be used to construct an endless series of wagers, choices among which yield a measure of value for all possible options and eventualities. It is then routine to calculate the degrees of belief in all propositions.

Ramsey was able to turn this trick by specifying constraints on the permissible patterns of simple preferences or choices. These constraints are not arbitrary, but are part of a satisfactory account of the reasons for a person's preferences and choice behavior. The constraints spell out the demand that an agent be rational, not in his particular and ultimate values, but in the pattern these form with one another and in combination with his beliefs. The theory thus has a strong normative element, but an element that is essential if the concepts of preference, belief, reason, and intentional action are to have application.

Pattern in what is observed is central to the intelligibility of an agent's choice behavior; it determines our ability to understand actions as done for a reason. The same pattern is central to the theory's power to extract, from facts that taken singly are relatively directly connected with what can be observed, facts of a more sophisticated kind (degree of belief, comparisons of differences in value).

From the point of view of the theory, the sophisticated facts explain the simple, more observable ones, while the observable ones constitute the evidential base for testing or applying the theory.

Bayesian decision theory does not provide a definition of the concepts of belief and preference on the basis of nonintensional notions. Rather, it makes use of one intensional notion, ordinal preference between gambles or outcomes, to give content to two further notions, degree of belief and comparisons of differences in value. So it would be a mistake to think the theory provides a reduction of intensional concepts to extensional concepts. Nevertheless, it is an important step in the direction of reducing complex and relatively theoretical intensional concepts to intensional concepts that in application are closer to publicly observable behavior. Above all, the theory shows how it is possible to assign a content to two basic and interlocking propositional attitudes without assuming that either one is understood in advance.

As a theory for explaining human actions, a Bayesian decision theory of the sort I have been describing is open to the criticism that it presupposes that we can identify and individuate the propositions to which attitudes like belief and desire (or preference) are directed. But as urged earlier, our ability to identify, and distinguish among, the propositions an agent entertains is not to be separated from our ability to understand what he says. We generally find out exactly what someone wants, prefers, or believes only by interpreting his speech. This is particularly obvious in the case of decision theory, where the objects to be chosen or preferred must often be complex wagers, with outcomes described as contingent on the occurrence of specific events. Clearly, a theory that attempts to elicit the attitudes and beliefs that explain preferences or choices must include a theory of verbal interpretation if it is not to make crippling assumptions.

What we must add to decision theory, or incorporate in it, then, is a theory of verbal interpretation, a way of telling what an agent means by his words. Yet this addition must be made in the absence of detailed information about the propositional contents of beliefs, desires, or intentions.

In important respects, Quine's approach to meaning is strikingly similar to Ramsey's approach to decision making. Noting that, while there is no direct way to observe what speakers mean, all the evidence required to implement communication must be publicly available, Quine surveys the relevant available evidence and asks how it could be used to elicit meanings. What can be observed, of course, is speech behavior in relation to the environment, and from this certain attitudes toward sentences can be fairly directly inferred, just as preferences can be inferred from choices. For Quine, the key observables are acts of *assent* and *dissent,* as caused by events within the ambit of the speaker and an audience. From such acts it is plausible to surmise that the speaker is caused by certain kinds of events to hold a sentence true.[11]

Just here a basic challenge arises. A speaker holds a sentence true as a result of two considerations: what he takes the sentence to mean, and what he believes to be the case. The problem is that what is relatively directly observable by an interpreter is the product of two unobservable attitudes, belief and meaning. How can the roles of these two explanatory factors be distinguished and extracted from the evidence? The problem is curiously like the problem of disentangling the roles of belief and preference in determining choices and preferences.

Quine's solution resembles Ramsey's, in principle if not in detail. The crucial step in both cases is to find a way to hold one factor steady in certain situations while determining the other. Quine's key idea is that the correct interpretation of an agent by another cannot intelligibly admit certain kinds and degrees of difference between

11. The step from observed assents to inferred attitude of holding true is not, I think, in Quine.

interpreter and interpreted with respect to belief. As a result, an interpreter is justified in making certain assumptions about the beliefs of an agent before interpretation begins. As a constraint on interpretation, this is often called by the name Neil Wilson gave it, the *principle of charity*.[12] As a device for separating meaning and belief without assuming either, it is a brilliant alternative to any approach to meaning that takes meanings for granted or assumes the analytic-synthetic distinction.

In what follows, I use Quine's method in ways that deviate, sometimes substantially, from his. A difference relevant to the present topic is this. Where Quine is concerned with the conditions of successful translation from a speaker's language into the interpreter's, I emphasize what the interpreter needs to know of the semantics of the speaker's language, that is, what is conveyed by the T-sentences entailed by a theory of truth. The relation between these two projects, Quine's and mine, is obvious: given a theory of truth for a speaker's language L stated in the interpreter's language M, it is fairly straightforward to produce a manual that translates (at least roughly) from L to M.[13] But the converse is false; there are many sentences we can translate without having any idea of how to incorporate them in a theory of truth. Demanding that a theory of interpretation satisfy the constraints of a theory of truth means that more structure than is needed for translation must be made manifest.

If we suppose, as the principle of charity says we unavoidably must, that the pattern of sentences to which a speaker assents reflects the semantics of the logical constants, it is possible to detect and interpret those constants. The guiding principles here, as in de-

12. Neil Wilson, "Substances without Substrata," *Review of Metaphysics* 12 (1959): 521–539.

13. The sailing may not be completely straight; it is easy to imagine a language which contains no translation of the English word 'now' but which can give the truth conditions of English sentences containing the word 'now'.

cision theory, derive from normative considerations. The relations between beliefs play a decisive constitutive role; an interpreter cannot accept great or obvious deviations from his own standards of rationality without destroying the foundation of intelligibility on which interpretation rests. The possibility of understanding the speech or actions of an agent depends on the existence of a fundamentally rational pattern, a pattern that must, in general outline, be shared by all rational creatures. We have no choice, then, but to project our own logic onto the language and beliefs of another. This means it is a constraint on possible interpretations of sentences held true that they are (within reason) logically consistent with one another.

Logical consistency yields no more than the interpretation of the logical constants, however (whatever we take to be the limits of logic and the list of logical constants). Further interpretation requires further forms of agreement between speaker and interpreter. Assuming that the identification of the logical constants required for first-order quantificational structure has been accomplished, it is possible to identify as such singular terms and predicates. This raises the question of how these are to be interpreted. Here progress depends on attending not just to which sentences an agent holds true, but also to the events and objects in the world that cause him to hold the sentences true. The circumstances, observable by speaker and interpreter alike, under which an agent is caused to accept as true sentences like 'It is raining,' 'That's a horse,' or 'My foot hurts,' provide the most obvious evidence for the interpretation of these sentences and the predicates in them. The interpreter, on noticing that the agent regularly accepts or rejects the sentence 'The coffee is ready' when the coffee is or is not ready, will (however tentatively pending related results) try for a theory of truth that says that an utterance by the agent of the sentence 'The coffee is ready' is true if and only if the coffee can be observed by the agent to be ready at the time of the utterance.

The interpretation of common predicates and names depends heavily on indexical elements in speech, such as demonstratives and tense, since it is these which most directly allow predicates and singular terms to be connected to objects and events in the world. (To accommodate indexical elements, theories of truth of the sort proposed by Tarski must be augmented; the nature of these modifications has been discussed elsewhere.)[14] The method I propose for interpreting the more observational sentences and predicates is similar in some respects to the method of Quine's *Word and Object* (§§7–10), but it differs in others. The most important difference concerns the objects or events that determine communicable content. For Quine, this is the patterns of nerve endings which prompt assent to a sentence; an observation sentence of a speaker is "stimulus synonymous" with an observation sentence of an interpreter if speaker and interpreter would be prompted to accept or reject their respective sentences by the same patterns of proximal stimulation. Quine's idea is to capture in respectably scientific form the empiricist idea that meaning depends on evidence directly available to each speaker. My approach, by contrast, is externalist: I suggest that interpretation depends (in the simplest and most basic situations) on the external objects and events salient to both speaker and interpreter, the very objects and events which the speaker's words are then taken by the interpreter to have as subject matter. It is the distal stimulus that matters to interpretation.[15] The significance of this point will be assessed presently.

The difficulty with what we may call the *distal theory of refer-*

14. The sort of modification required is discussed in my *Inquiries into Truth and Interpretation.*

15. I have discussed this aspect of Quine's theory of meaning in "Meaning, Truth, and Evidence," in *Perspectives on Quine,* ed. R. Gibson (New York: Blackwell, 1989). There I note that Quine also sometimes seems to subscribe to the "distal" theory, particularly in *The Roots of Reference* (La Salle, Ill.: Open Court, 1973). [Note added, 2003: Quine later accepted the distal view in "Progress on Two Fronts," *Journal of Philosophy* 93 (1996): 159–163.]

ence is that it makes error hard to explain—the crucial gap between what is believed true and what is true; since the distal theory directly relates truth to belief, the problem is crucial. The solution depends on two closely related interpretive devices. An interpreter bent on working out a speaker's meanings notes more than what causes assents and dissents; he notes how well placed and equipped the speaker is to observe aspects of her environment, and accordingly gives more weight to some verbal responses than to others. This provides him with the rudiments of an explanation of deviant cases where the speaker calls a sheep a goat because she is mistaken about the animal rather than the word. The subtler and more important device depends on the interanimation of sentences. By this I mean the extent to which a speaker counts the truth of one sentence as supporting the truth of others. We have seen an example of how evidence of such dependencies leads to the interpretation of logical constants. But matters of evidential support can also aid in the interpretation of so-called observational terms, by helping to explain error.

The interpretation of terms less directly keyed to untutored observation must also depend in large measure on conditional probabilities, which show what the agent counts as evidence for the application of his more theoretical predicates. If we want to identify and so interpret the role of a theoretical concept or its linguistic expression, we must know how it relates to other concepts and words. These relations are in general holistic and probabilistic. We can therefore spot them only if we can detect the degree to which an agent holds a sentence true, his subjective probabilities. Simple assent and dissent are at extreme and opposite ends of a scale; we need to be able to locate attitudes that are intermediate in strength. Degree of belief, however, cannot be directly diagnosed by an interpreter; as we saw in discussing decision theory, degree of belief is a construction based on more elementary attitudes.

The theory of verbal interpretation and Bayesian decision theory are evidently made for each other. Decision theory must be freed from the assumption of independent access to meanings; theory of meaning calls for a theory of degree of belief in order to make serious use of relations of evidential support. But stating these mutual dependencies is not enough, for neither theory can be developed first as a basis for the other. There is no way simply to add one to the other, since in order to get started each requires an element drawn from the other. What is wanted is a unified theory that yields degree of belief, desirabilities on an interval scale, and an interpretation of speech, a theory that does not assume that either desires or beliefs have been individuated in advance, much less quantified.

Such a theory must be based on some simple attitude that an interpreter can recognize in an agent before the interpreter has detailed knowledge of any of the agent's propositional attitudes. The following attitude will serve: the attitude an agent has toward two of his sentences when he prefers the truth of one to the truth of the other. The sentences must be endowed with meaning by the speaker, of course, but interpreting the sentences is part of the interpreter's task. What the interpreter has to go on, then, is information about what episodes and situations in the world cause an agent to prefer that one rather than another sentence be true. Clearly an interpreter can know this without knowing what the sentences mean, what states of affairs the agent values, or what he believes. But the preferring true of one sentence to another by an agent is equally clearly a function of what the agent takes the sentences to mean, the value he sets on various possible or actual states of the world, and the probability he attaches to those states contingent on the truth of the relevant sentences. So it is not absurd to think that all three attitudes of the agent can be abstracted from the pattern of an agent's preferences among sentences.

It may be objected that a preference for the truth of one sentence rather than another is itself an intentional state, and one that could be known to hold only on the assumption that many psychological factors are present. This is true (as it is also of assent to, or the holding true of, a sentence). But the objective was not to avoid intentional states; it was to avoid *individualized* intentional states, *intensional* states, states with (as one says) a propositional object. A preference for the truth of one sentence over another is an extensional relation that relates an agent and two sentences (and a time). Because it can be detected without knowing what the sentences mean, a theory of interpretation based on it can hope to make the crucial step from the nonpropositional to the propositional.

Here, in outline, is how I think the hope can be satisfied. We have already seen (again in survey form) how to arrive at a theory of meaning and belief on the basis of knowledge about the degrees to which sentences are held true. So if we could derive degree of belief in sentences by appeal to information about preferences that sentences be true, we would have a successful unified theory.

Ramsey's version of Bayesian decision theory makes essential use of gambles or wagers, and this creates a difficulty for my project. For how can we tell that an agent views a sentence as presenting a gamble until we are far along in the process of interpreting his language? A gamble, after all, specifies a connection, presumably causal, between the occurrence of a certain event (a coin comes up heads) and a specific outcome (you win a horse). Even assuming we could tell when an agent accepts such a connection, straightforward application of the theory depends also on the causing event (the coin coming up heads) having no value, negative or positive, in itself. It is also necessary to assume that the probability the agent assigns to the coin coming up heads is not contaminated by thoughts about the likelihood of winning a horse. In experimental tests of decision theory, one tries to provide environments in which these assumptions have a chance of being true; but the general application we now have in mind cannot be so choosy.

We owe to Richard Jeffrey a version of Bayesian decision theory

that makes no direct use of gambles, but treats the objects of preference, the objects to which subjective probabilities are assigned, and
the objects to which relative values are assigned all as propositions.[16] Jeffrey has shown in detail how to extract subjective probabilities and values from preferences that propositions be true.

An obvious problem remains. Jeffrey shows how to get results
much like Ramsey's by substituting preferences among propositions
for preferences among gambles. But if we know the propositions an
agent is choosing among, our original problem of interpreting language and individuating propositional attitudes is assumed to have
been solved from the start. What we want is to get Jeffrey's results,
but starting with preferences among *uninterpreted* sentences, not
propositions.

This turns out to be a soluble problem, given appropriate assumptions. Jeffrey's method for finding the subjective probabilities
and relative desirabilities of propositions depends on only the truth-
functional structure of propositions—on how propositions are
made up out of simple propositions by repeated application of conjunction, disjunction, negation, and the other operations definable
in terms of these. If we start with sentences instead of proposi-

16. Richard Jeffrey, *The Logic of Decision,* 2nd ed. (Chicago: University of
Chicago Press, 1983). Jeffrey's theory does not determine probabilities and util-
ities up to the same sets of transformations as standard theories. Instead of a
utility function determined up to a linear transformation, in Jeffrey's theory
the utility function is unique only up to a fractional linear transformation; and
the probability assignments, instead of being unique once a number is chosen
for measuring certainty (always One), are unique only to within a certain
quantization. These diminutions in determinacy are conceptually and practi-
cally appropriate: they amount, among other things, to permitting somewhat
the same sort of indeterminacy in decision theory that we have come to expect
in a theory of linguistic interpretation. Just as it is possible to account for the
same data in decision theory using various utility functions by making corresponding changes in the probability function, so you can change the meanings
you attribute to a person's words (within limits) provided you make compensat-
ing changes in the beliefs you attribute to him.

tions, then the crucial difficulty will be overcome provided the truth-functional connectives can be identified. For once these connectives have been identified, Jeffrey has shown how to fix, to the desired degree, the subjective desirabilities and probabilities of all sentences; and this, I have argued, suffices to yield a theory for interpreting the sentences. Knowing an agent's evaluative and cognitive attitudes to interpreted sentences is not (at least in the context of this approach) to be distinguished from knowing the agent's beliefs and desires.

The basic empirical primitive in the method to be described is the agent's (weak) preference that one sentence rather than another be true; one may therefore think of the data as being of the same sort as the data usually gathered in an experimental test of any Bayesian theory of decision, with the proviso that the interpretation of the sentences among which the agent chooses is not assumed to be known in advance to the experimenter or interpreter.

The uniformity and simplicity of the empirical ontology of the system, comprising as it does just utterances and sentences, is essential to achieving the aim of combining decision theory with interpretation. I shall follow Jeffrey, whose theory deals with propositions only, as closely as possible, substituting uninterpreted sentences where he assumes propositions. Here, then, is the analogue of Jeffrey's *desirability axiom* (D), applied to sentences rather than propositions:

(D) If $prob(s \text{ and } t) = 0$ and $prob(s \text{ or } t) \neq 0$, then

$$des(s \text{ or } t) = \frac{prob(s)des(s) + prob(t)des(t)}{prob(s) + prob(t)}$$

(I write '$prob(s)$' for the subjective probability of s and '$des(s)$' for the desirability or utility of s.) By relating preference and belief, this axiom does the sort of work usually done by gambles; the relation is, however, different. Events are identified with sentences which on interpretation turn out to say that the event occurs ('The next card is a club'). Actions and outcomes are also represented by sentences ('The agent bets one dollar,' 'The agent wins five dollars'). Gambles do not enter directly, but the element of risk is present, since to choose that a sentence be true is usually to take a risk on what will concomitantly be true. (It is assumed that one cannot choose a logically false sentence.) So we see that if the agent chooses to make true rather than false the sentence 'The agent bets one dollar,' he is taking a chance on the outcome, which may, for example, be thought to depend on whether or not the next card is a club. Then the desirability of (the truth of) the sentence 'The agent bets one dollar' will be the desirability of the various circumstances in which this sentence is true weighted in the usual way by the probabilities of those circumstances. Suppose the agent believes he will win five dollars if the next card is a club and will win nothing if the next card is not a club; he will then have a special interest in whether the truth of 'The agent bets one dollar' will be paired with the truth or falsity of 'The next card is a club.' Let these two sentences be abbreviated by 's' and 't'. Then

$$des(s) = \frac{prob(s \text{ and } t)des(s \text{ and } t) + prob(s \text{ and } \sim t)des(s \text{ and } \sim t)}{prob(s)}$$

This is, of course, something like Ramsey's gambles. It differs, however, in that there is no assumption that the "states of nature" that may be thought to determine outcomes are, in Ramsey's term, "morally neutral," that is, have no effect on the desirabilities of the outcomes. Nor is there the assumption that the probabilities of outcomes depend on nothing but the probabilities of the "states of nature" (the agent may believe he has a chance of winning five dollars even if the next card is not a club, and a chance he will not win five dollars even if the next card is a club).

The "desirability axiom" (D) can be used to show how probabilities depend on desirabilities in Jeffrey's system. Take the special case where $t = \sim s$. Then we have

(1) $\qquad des(s \text{ or } \sim s) = des(s)prob(s) + des(\sim s)prob(\sim s)$

Since $prob(s) + prob(\sim s) = 1$, we can solve for $prob(s)$:

(2) $\qquad prob(s) = \dfrac{des(s \text{ or } \sim s) - des(\sim s)}{des(s) - des(\sim s)}$

In words, the probability of a proposition depends on the desirability of that proposition and of its negation. Further, it is easy to see that if a sentence s is more desirable than an arbitrary logical truth (such as 't or $\sim t$'), then its negation ('$\sim s$') cannot also be more desirable than a logical truth. Suppose that (with Jeffrey) we assign the number 0 to any logical truth. (This is intuitively reasonable since an agent is indifferent to the truth of a tautology.) Then (2) can be rewritten:

(3) $\qquad prob(s) = \dfrac{1}{1 - \dfrac{des(s)}{des(\sim s)}}$

It is at once apparent that $des(s)$ and $des(\sim s)$ cannot both be more, or both be less, desirable than 0, the desirability of any logical truth, if $prob(s)$ is to fall in the interval from 1 to 0. If (once again following Jeffrey) we call an option good if it is preferred to a logical truth and bad if a logical truth is preferred to it, then (3) shows that it is impossible for an option (sentence) and its negation both to be good or both to be bad.

Taking '$\sim(s \text{ and } \sim s)$' as our sample logical truth, we can state this principle purely in terms of preferences:

(4) $\qquad$ If $des(s) > des(\sim(s \text{ and } \sim s))$ then

$\qquad\qquad des(\sim(s \text{ and } \sim s)) \geq des(\sim s)$, and

$$\text{if } des(\sim(s \text{ and } \sim s)) > des(s) \text{ then}$$

$$des(\sim s) \geq des(\sim(s \text{ and } \sim s)).$$

Since both negation and conjunction can be defined in terms of the Sheffer stroke '|' ("not both"), (4) can be rewritten:

(5)   If $des(s) > des((t|u)|((t|u)|(t|u)))$ then

$$des((t|u)|((t|u)|(t|u))) \geq des(s|s), \text{ and}$$

if $des((t|u)|((t|u)|(t|u))) > des(s)$ then

$$des(s|s) \geq ((des((t|u)|((t|u)|(t|u)))).$$

The interest of (5) for present purposes is this. If we assume that '|' is some arbitrary truth-functional operator that forms sentences out of pairs of sentences, then the following holds: if (5) is true for all sentences s, t, and u, and for some s and t, $des(s|s) \neq des(t|t)$, then '|' must be the Sheffer stroke (it must have the logical properties of "not both"); no other interpretation is possible.

Thus data involving only preferences among sentences, the meanings of which are unknown to the interpreter, has led (given the constraints of the theory) to the identification of one sentential connective. Since all logically equivalent sentences are equal in desirability, it is now possible to interpret all the other truth-functional sentential connectives, since all are definable in terms of the Sheffer stroke. For example, if it is found that, for all sentences s,

$$des(s|s) = des(\sim s),$$

we can conclude that the tilde is the sign for negation.

It is now possible to measure the desirability and subjective probability of all sentences, for the application of formulas like (2) and (3) requires the identification of only the truth-functional sentential connectives. Thus it is clear from (3) that if two sentences are equal in desirability (and are preferred to a logical truth) and their negations are also equal in desirability, the sentences must have the same probability. By the same token, if two sentences are equal in desirability (and are preferred to a logical truth), but the negation of one is preferred to the negation of the other, then the probability of the first is less than that of the second. This, along with appropriate existence axioms, is enough to establish a probability scale. Then it is easy to determine the relative desirabilities of all sentences.

At this point the probabilities and desirabilities of all sentences have in theory been determined. But no complete sentence has yet been interpreted, although the truth-functional sentential connectives have been identified, and so sentences that are logically true or false by virtue of sentential logic can be recognized.

We have shown how to interpret the simplest sentences on the basis of (degrees of) belief in their truth, however. Given degrees of belief and the relative strengths of desire for the truth of interpreted sentences, we can give a propositional content to the beliefs and desires of an agent.

How? An empirical theory is outlined which relates belief, desire, and meaning to one another, and a sketch (radical interpretation) is given of what is required of an interpreter to judge when the theory holds of a speaker. Among other things, the speaker must employ his own beliefs, what he holds true. So, one can say *the* concept of truth is essential to understanding others and explaining why they act as they do.

The approach to the problems of meaning, belief, and desire which I have outlined is not, I am sure it is clear, meant to throw any direct light on how in real life we come to understand each other, nor on how we master our first concepts and our first language.[17] I have been engaged in a conceptual exercise aimed at re-

17. Given the intricacy of any interpretable system of thought and language, I assume that there must be many alternative approaches to interpretation. I have outlined one; others may well be less artificial or closer to our intuitions concerning interpretive practice. But one should not take for granted that the

vealing the dependencies among our basic propositional attitudes at a level fundamental enough to avoid the assumption that we can come to grasp them, or intelligibly attribute them to others, one at a time. Performing the exercise has required showing how it is in principle possible to arrive at all of them at once. Showing this amounts to presenting an informal proof that we have endowed thought, desire, and speech with a structure that makes interpretation possible. Of course, we knew this was possible in advance. The philosophical question was, what makes it possible?

What makes the task practicable at all is the structure that the normative character of thought, desire, speech, and action imposes on correct attributions of attitudes to others, and hence on interpretations of their speech and explanations of their actions. What I have said about the norms that govern our theories of intensional attribution is crude, vague, and incomplete. The way to improve our understanding of such understanding is to improve our grasp of the standards of rationality implicit in all interpretation of thought and action.

The idea that the propositional content of observation sentences is (in most cases) determined by what is common and salient to both speaker and interpreter is a direct correlate of the common-sense view of language learning. It has profound consequences for the relation between thought and meaning, and for our view of the role of truth, for it ensures not only that there is a ground level on which speakers largely share views, but also that what they share is a largely correct picture of a common world. The ultimate source of

procedure I have sketched is totally remote from what is practicable. As a start, observe that every utterance that can be treated as a sincere request or demand may be taken to express the utterer's preference that a certain sentence be true rather than its negation. Most experimental work in decision theory takes as data the choices that subjects make between alternatives as described in writing or speech. It is normally assumed that subjects understand these descriptions as the experimenters do. Dropping this assumption yields data of exactly the sort required by the approach presented here.

both objectivity and communication is the triangle that, by relating speaker, interpreter, and the world, determines the contents of thought and speech. Given this source, there is no room for a relativized concept of truth.

We recognized that truth must somehow be related to the attitudes of rational creatures; this relation is now revealed as springing from the nature of interpersonal understanding. Linguistic communication, the indispensable instrument of fine-grained interpersonal understanding, rests on mutually understood utterances, the contents of which are finally fixed by the patterns and causes of sentences held true. The conceptual underpinning of interpretation is a theory of truth; truth thus rests in the end on belief and, even more ultimately, on the affective attitudes.[18]

18. [Davidson noted that the following points should be incorporated in Chapter 2 or 3: "It isn't obvious, though, that I am right to assume that if correspondence fails, some form of epistemic theory must be right. But it *is* my view that if deflation and correspondence fail, some form of epistemic view is right. By this I mean there is an essential connection between truth and belief." (Charles Parsons comments: "In the second chapter Davidson says flatly that epistemic views are false, and he does not change that. But in this paragraph he seems to use the phrase 'some form of epistemic view' to include his own view, for example as laid out in this chapter. Davidson sees this issue as bound up with 'the concept of truth.' About epistemic views, the general idea is that he admits that there is an 'essential connection' between truth and belief, but denies that truth is reduced to warranted belief or assertion or one of the constructs from those concepts that have been advocated, such as Peirce's idea of what would be accepted at an ideal end of inquiry.")

Davidson's note continues: "Does it make sense to talk of *the* concept of truth? Well, since one isn't doing semantics, the answer is 'No.' It must always be relativized to a language. First we go to utterances (or as a substitute, sentences relativized in various ways, to a language, a person).

"I want to make clear that my 'solution' isn't a basic one. It is an alternative to deflationary, epistemological correspondence theories not in proposing a better *definition* (or short summary) but in suggesting a different approach which relates the concept of truth to other concepts."]

CHAPTER 4

The Problem of Predication

Arabic is an economical language: a sentence can get along without an explicit verb. One can say, in effect, 'Man mortal', or 'Today rainy', or 'John sad'. This feature of Arabic recently led to a political tempest in Egypt. A book was banned because a review suggested that the author had written "The Koran bad." The words were spoken by a character in a novel by the Syrian author Haida Haidar, but the reviewer had omitted three little dots between the subject and the adjective. The original context had made clear that Haida had not intended what in English would have been supplied by the word 'is'.[1] Confusion about predication can create problems; one of those problems concerns the copula or its absence.

In English, 'John mortal' is not a sentence. It becomes one if the word 'is' is inserted between noun and adjective. This is a fact of syntax or grammar. But what is the semantic role of the copula? This question and related questions about the nature of predication have been evident since Plato. Yet despite the earnest regard which the semantics of natural languages has attracted over the years, no one who was aware of the problem has come up with a satisfactory account of predication. Or, to put the point more accurately, a satis-

---

1. Max Rodenbeck, "Witch Hunt in Egypt," *New York Review of Books,* November 16, 2000, pp. 39–42.

factory account exists, but apparently no one has noticed that this account solves the problem. This chapter and those that follow are about fragments of the history of the problem from Plato up to the present, and its solution, unrecognized as such, almost seventy years ago.

The topic should attract our attention. After all, if we do not understand predication, we do not understand how any sentence works, nor can we account for the structure of the simplest thought that is expressible in language. At one time there was much discussion of what was called the "unity of the proposition"; it is just this unity that a theory of predication must explain. The philosophy of language lacks its most important chapter without such a theory; the philosophy of mind is missing a crucial first step if it cannot describe the nature of judgment; and it is woeful if metaphysics cannot say how a substance is related to its attributes.

Plato is mainly responsible for introducing the problem of predication; the theory of forms or ideas led directly to it. We may think of the problem as a metaphysical one by asking: How are particulars related to universals? Alternatively, we may ask the semantical question: How are names or other singular terms related to predicates? Plato discusses both questions; indeed, it is only now and then that he distinguishes between them. Aristotle carries on the discussion, and the problem continued to plague philosophers and logicians throughout the Middle Ages. In recent times the issue has tended to be viewed primarily as a problem in the philosophy of language, and I shall for the most part follow this tendency. But I follow it only because the problem can be stated so clearly in semantical terms and not because I think metaphysics and semantics are unrelated disciplines. Certainly not in the case of predication.

The Socratic dialogues, like *Euthyphro, Charmides, Laches,* and *Greater Hippias,* ask what it is that "makes" a man, or one of his actions, pious, courageous, wise, or virtuous. The question is obscure until we find out what Socrates rejects as an answer. Seeking the nature of courage, he will not accept a list of examples of brave acts as an answer, since the list assumes we know what courage is, but it does not tell us what it is the examples have in common. He also will not accept as an answer a concept that fails to explain why an act is brave, even if it applies to all and only brave acts. Thus in the *Euthyphro* Socrates rejects the suggestion that what makes an act holy is that it is dear to the gods, even though all and only holy acts are dear to the gods. He argues that an act is not holy because it is dear to the gods, but that it is dear to the gods because it is holy.

Gregory Vlastos thinks that Socrates' interest in these dialogues is "purely definitional."[2] What is to be defined is in each case a single form or idea (εἶδος, ἰδέα), and Socrates is clear that the forms exist. This is, as Vlastos says, a "substantial ontological commitment."[3] The forms are not like particular physical objects; they are unchanging, and where the objects that exhibit a form are typically many, the form thus exhibited is a unit. Since the forms are clearly not the sort of thing that can be seen or handled, the Socrates who is portrayed in the early dialogues assumes that there are two very different sorts of entity. Though these dialogues do not explicitly argue for it, this ontological dualism is repeatedly emphasized. In subsequent dialogues, arguments for the existence of the forms emerge, difficulties are discussed, and many further characteristics of the forms are suggested. But although the forms are treated as unproblematic in the early dialogues, it is easy to discern two problems about predication which were to occupy a large place in Plato's later thinking. One problem is how the forms are related to their instantiations. The other is how the forms are related to one another.

In one dialogue or another Plato tells us that the forms are not perceived by the senses, but are objects of the mind; that they are

2. Gregory Vlastos, *Socrates* (Cambridge: Cambridge University Press, 1991), p. 56.

3. Ibid., p. 57.

imperishable; that they are indivisible; that they are superior to material objects; that they are norms by which we judge material things; that they have a certain creative power (the form of wisdom "makes" Socrates wise). Material objects participate in, resemble, copy, or are modeled by the forms. Problems arise because some of these characteristics of the forms turn out to clash with others. If material things resemble the forms they instantiate to various degrees, then material things have something in common with any form they resemble. If a well-drawn circle resembles the form of circularity, it must be because both the particular drawn circle and the form of circularity share the property of circularity; but then what the particular and the property share must be still another form. Scholars of Plato have puzzled over this problem, the problem of the "third man," because it seems to lead to an infinite regress. If Plato did fall into a difficulty here, it is due to an error which he seems later to have overcome. It is a mistake to think that shapes have a shape, that colors have a color, or that Socrates resembles the concept or idea of a man. Material objects are created, change, and perish. They occupy space and exist in time. None of these characteristics apply to the forms according to Plato. But although this difficulty is easy to evade simply by giving up the idea that particulars resemble, or are copies of, the forms they instantiate, infinite regress infects many views of predication from Plato's time to today. The difficulty of avoiding one infinite regress or another might almost be said to be *the* problem of predication, as will become clear.

Another serious problem for Plato was generated by his view that the forms are models which constitute a norm for institutions, material particulars, and ways of behaving: the more like a form one of these entities is, the more valuable it is. This notion is of central importance in the *Republic* and other dialogues close in date. Later, however, Plato seems to have abandoned both the idea that particulars resemble the forms they instantiate and the view that the forms are norms. In the *Parmenides,* for example, Parmenides suggests to young Socrates that when he grows up he will admit forms of all kinds of objects. This admission becomes necessary as Plato evolves the method of collection and division in the *Sophist* and *Politicus.* The method of division, which means specifying the species that fall under a genus, the sub-species that fall under a species, and so on down to the infima species, often creates categories of worthless or evil particulars. In the *Philebus,* for example, pleasures are divided into those that are of positive value and those that should be excluded from the good life. Another example is provided by the various categories into which sophists are placed. Taking art as the genus, the Stranger in the *Sophist* first distinguishes acquisitive and productive arts. The acquisitive arts then divide into those that acquire by exchange and those that acquire by capture. The arts that acquire by exchange then subdivide into no less than three categories, in each of which the sophist may be found: merchants, retailers, and salesmen of information. But the sophist also falls into the class of hunters, for he is a hunter of rich young men. After adding the category of those who practice eristic, the Stranger points out that the sophist appears in so many guises that he really should be called an imitator who creates the illusion of truth and wisdom.

This slightly tongue-in-cheek characterization of the sophist raises the question of how it is possible to say or think "what is not." To say "what is not" is impossible according to Parmenides, since there would be no subject matter for the saying. If this is so, the sophist need not worry about the accusation of peddling falsehoods. The Stranger takes up the challenge to explain how we can think and say what is false. He considers two sentences, 'Theaetetus sits' and 'Theaetetus flies', one true and one false.[4] These short sen-

4. In the *Sophist* Plato distinguishes between thought and speech, but insists that with respect to the question of how false thoughts or sentences are possible, what applies to one applies to the other (260A/C). "Our power of discourse is derived from the interweaving of the forms with one another" (259E).

tences have two parts: the Stranger calls them name (ὄνομα) and verb (ῥῆμα). Each of these parts, according to the Stranger, corresponds to something that exists. In our sample sentences the relevant entities are Theaetetus and the forms Sitting and Flying. As a consequence, the first sentence is true because there is the compound fact of Theaetetus sitting. But there is no fact that corresponds to 'Theaetetus flies', for Theaetetus is not flying. Nevertheless, each of the components to which the words 'Theaetetus' and 'flies' correspond does exist, and so the sentence is perfectly intelligible. This shows that there is no reason why we cannot understand the assertion or the judgment that Theaetetus flies. This is so even though there is a sense in which the sentence as a whole is "about" something that does not exist.[5]

In the course of distinguishing names and verbs, the Stranger makes a portentous claim: a sentence must contain both a noun and a verb. 'Lion stag horse' is not a sentence, nor is 'Walks runs sleeps'. A sentence must have a word that picks out an object, and a verb that picks out a general form. In our examples, 'Theaetetus' picks out the individual Theaetetus and 'sits' and 'flies' stand for properties or forms which Theaetetus may or may not exemplify. In the *Sophist* Plato uses a number of expressions for the relation between words and the entities they stand for, name, or indicate. To the annoyance of scholars, the theory of forms is not explicitly invoked at this point in the *Sophist*. The reason for this is unclear. But the explanation of the meaningfulness of false statements is more cogent if many of the attributes that have been assigned to the forms are dropped.

In the late dialogues, but particularly in these passages in the *Sophist,* the problem of predication becomes clearer as distinctions necessary for its solution emerge. The partial explanation of how false statements are intelligible depends on the recognition of three

5. The examples and discussion are in *Sophist* 261D–264B.

essential aspects of any judgment or sentence that can be used to express a judgment. These are, first, that the judgment or sentence must in some way constitute a unity; its parts must fit together to produce something that can be true or false. The second is that every sentence must contain a verb and one or more elements that determine a "subject matter." The third is that these two elements must be very different in function.

Although these points are relatively clearly stated in the *Sophist,* it cannot be said that Plato develops them systematically, or even that he keeps them in mind in the rest of the dialogue. Consider the discussion of how the forms are related to each other. The question is how to think of sentences like 'Motion is not Rest'. This does not deny existence to either Motion or Rest, but it does tell us that the two forms, both of which exist, are not identical; to refute Parmenides, Plato here distinguishes between the 'is' of existence and the 'is' of identity (*Sophist* 255B,C). The relations of the forms to each other are immutable, Plato says, since a form does not change; in this respect the relation of one form to another differs from the relation of a material particular to the various forms in which it participates, for the latter relations can change. Plato speaks of the forms as blending, connecting, or mixing with one another. In the case of Rest and Motion, they fail to blend. The difficulty is to reconcile these declarations with the claim that every sentence must have a verb. Clearly the words 'Motion' and 'Rest' name or refer to forms, so if the sentence 'Motion is not Rest' has a verb, it must be 'is' or 'is not' (or 'blends with' or 'does not blend with'). Plato takes Sameness and Difference to be forms, but then fails to recognize that if these forms are what is meant by the 'is' and 'is not' in sentences that speak of the forms blending or failing to blend, then a sentence like 'Motion is not Rest' names three forms ('Motion Difference Rest'?), and there is no verb.

If Identity and Difference are not verbs but names of forms, then the same must hold of 'sits' and 'flies'; they should be 'Sits' and

'Flies'. Both 'Theaetetus sits' and 'Motion is not Rest' lack a verb. How could Plato have failed to notice this? Part of the answer may be that Plato, like Aristotle, did not have the concept of a relation as holding *between* two entities; what we think of as a relation, he thought of as a special case of a property. Motion is different with respect to Rest, and Rest is different with respect to Motion (Difference is a property that every form has with respect to every other).[6] Of course, 'Motion is not x' and 'x is not Rest' are one-place predicates. However, this observation is of no help as long as one holds that predicates refer to forms. But we have been told that every sentence must contain a verb.

There are various ways in which one might attempt to reconcile the apparent contradictions or explain the inadequacies in Plato's accounts of predication, but it would be inappropriate to pursue the matter here. What is of present interest is that Plato, goaded perhaps by Parmenides, introduced the problem to Western philosophy, and made available some of the most important distinctions relevant to solving it. It is a mark of Plato's extraordinary philosophical power that he introduced a problem that remained unresolved for more than two millennia.

What, then, is the problem? There is the metaphysical question of how particulars are related to properties, and the semantical question of how subjects and predicates are related. Plato raised the question in both of its guises, but both the question and proffered partial solutions are obscured by metaphor, analogical reasoning, irony, and myth making. The first task is to try to get clearer about the problem, or problems, so that we are in a position to recognize when a suggested solution is satisfactory, and when it is not.

It may seem relatively easy to answer the metaphysical question. The judgment that Theaetetus sits, for example, relates Theaetetus

6. Cornford makes this point in *Plato's Theory of Knowledge* (London: Routledge, 1960), p. 284, and he reminds us that in the *Categories* Aristotle included among predicates 'in the Lyceum' and 'yesterday.'

to the property of being seated. The relation between Theaetetus and the property is that of instantiation. To put it more plainly, we can say that Theaetetus *has* the property. We can extend the idea to judgments about the relations among properties. Thus the judgment that the property Motion differs from the property Rest relates two entities which are equally the subject of the judgment. Here the idea of a property is replaced by that of a relation, the relation of Difference, or non-identity. The idea that relations are just as basic as properties was, of course, a long time coming. But let us accept the fact that here Plato was *directly* faced with a relation, and a relation that he considered at length, calling it, as we have seen, the relation of blending, mixing, or failing to mix (as in the case of Motion and Rest). I emphasize the directness of the confrontation because there is a difference between the case where there is a word or phrase, verbal in character, which expresses the relation ('Motion differs from (or is not) Rest') when we put the judgment into words, and cases where the presence of a relation is not evident, as in the judgment that Theaetetus sits.

At this point we are forced to recognize that properties and relations are playing two entirely different roles in the account of judgments like the judgment that Motion differs from Rest. The properties of Motion and Rest constitute the subject matter of the judgment, while the relation of Difference is not part of the subject matter but instead is the relation judged to hold between the two properties. We could say that the relation of Difference is needed to explain the verbal element in the judgment. There is still another way we might put this point: in the judgment that Motion and Rest differ, the fact that Motion and Rest are universals is, so to speak, passive, while the universal character of the concept of Difference is active.

There is no objection to taking properties and relations as entities about which we want to think and say things, unless, of course, there are no such entities. I shall not cast doubt on their existence:

the question of whether they exist will play no part in what follows. The more basic question is whether positing the existence of properties and relations helps us to understand the structure and nature of judgments like the judgment that Theaetetus sits or that Motion is different from Rest. Let us take one more look. Theaetetus sits. Theaetetus, we agree, is an entity, a person. He is sitting. The property of Sitting is another entity, this time a universal that can be instantiated by many particular entities. In the present case, Theaetetus is one of those entities. In other words, we explain what it is for it to be the case that Theaetetus sits by saying that Theaetetus instantiates the property of Sitting. The fact itself doesn't, then, consist merely of the two entities, Theaetetus and the property of Sitting. It is a fact because those two entities stand in a certain relation to each other, the relation of Instantiation. We learned, from the example of the judgment that Motion differs from Rest, that we must take relations as seriously as we take properties. Now we see that a fact we can describe in just two words apparently involves three entities. But can 'Theaetetus sits' consist of just the three entities, Theaetetus, Sitting, and Instantiation? Surely not. The fact requires as well that these three entities stand in a certain relation to one another: Theaetetus and Sitting, in that order, bear the relation of Instantiation to one another. To explain this fact we need to mention this *fourth* entity, which, unlike Instantiation, is a three-place relation. We are clearly off on an infinite regress.

The problem is easier to state in semantical terms, and Plato gave us what we need to recognize it as a problem when he said that a sentence could not consist of a string of names or a string of verbs. The sentence 'Theaetetus sits' has a word that refers to, or names, Theaetetus, and a word whose function is somehow explained by mentioning the property (or form or universal) of Sitting. But the sentence says that Theaetetus *has* this property. If the semantics of the sentence were exhausted by referring to the two entities Theaetetus and the property of Sitting, it would be just a string of names; we would ask where the verb was. The verb, we understand, expresses the relation of instantiation. Our policy, however, is to explain verbs by relating them to properties and relations. But this cannot be the end of the matter, since we now have three entities, a person, a property, and a relation, but no verb. When we supply the appropriate verb, we will be forced to the next step, and so on. This is one of the several ways in which the problem of predication may be posed.

I have been depending, in these remarks, on the intuitive appeal of the idea that we can use a sentence to say something. This works if one feels that it is right that saying something cannot be a matter of simply referring, or somehow adverting, to one or more entities. It is of no help to insist that the entities named must be of very different kinds—witness the sentence 'Motion differs from Rest'. Nor can the difficulty be overcome by distinguishing two ways in which a word can be related to an entity. We might think that names *refer* to entities, while verbs *relate* properties or relations to the entities named. But the apparent asymmetry between names and verbs which this view suggests breaks down when we realize that the relation of a name to what it names is something we must know to understand the name, not something *expressed* by the sentence, whereas the relation of a property or a relation to the entity or entities named must be expressed by the sentence. In any case, the purported asymmetry does not explain the relation between the thing named and the property.

Does the problem of predication necessarily rest on the intuitive, but vague and ambiguous, concept of what is required of a sentence if it is to "say something"? The right answer is, I think, that the problem can be stated more directly and clearly by asking instead what is required of a sentence if it is to be true or false. Perhaps not every sentence has a truth value, but surely many do. When the Stranger of the *Sophist* uttered the sentence 'Theaetetus sits' (or rather 'Θεαίτητος κάθηται'), the sentence was either true or false.

To understand the sentence, it is necessary to know under what conditions it would be true. The sentence 'Theaetetus sits' is true if it is uttered when Theaetetus is sitting. What is the role of the words in the sentence that explains this? Well, the name 'Theaetetus' must name someone, and in this case it does name Theaetetus. What is the role of the verb or predicate? If we say it names or is otherwise related to the property of Sitting, we have so far pointed to nothing that could be true or false, for we have simply indicated two entities. Of course what we want to add is that the sentence is true if and only if the entity named *has* the property: Theaetetus has the property of Sitting. The little word 'has' is the missing verb: it is a two-place predicate which should, in turn, be explained by reference to the relation of Instantiation. We are off once more on the regress.

Clearly, what the problem of predication is concerned with is none other than an example of what is often called the unity of the proposition. Sentences express propositions, which is why the unity of the proposition guarantees the unity of the sentence. Some philosophers like to think of propositions as the meanings of the sentences that express them, in which case we could also speak of the unity of the meaning of a sentence. Bearing in mind the distinction between meaning and reference, we can also speak of the truth value of a sentence as a sign of the unity of a sentence: only whole sentences have a truth value. Though these may appear to be different forms that the problem of predication can take, it will turn out that each form has an obvious translation into the other forms. It will also turn out that a solution to the problem of predication will account for all the ways in which we conceive the unity of the sentence and the proposition it expresses.

Though Plato was aware of the problem of predication, he did not resolve it to his own satisfaction. He also realized that the problem was of great importance to philosophy; otherwise it would be impossible to understand why he devoted so much space to one aspect or another of the problem in the *Parmenides,* the *Sophist,* the *Politicus,* and the *Philebus.* I do not mention the earlier dialogues in which the theory of forms is developed and put to work, nor the *Timaeus,* which again is not concerned with the problems raised by the forms.

We know, mainly from Aristotle, that the forms were much discussed in the Academy, but the information that Aristotle vouchsafes on the contents of the disputes surrounding the theory, and the defenses of the theory, is much colored by his own criticisms. Aristotle criticized the theory often and with vigor. Some of his criticisms are directed against views that so far as we know Plato never held, and others deal with views that were explicitly rejected by Plato. There is much dispute among the experts as to whether Aristotle means to discuss views that Plato expressed in the *Philebus* with respect to what Plato there calls the limit and the unlimited. For present purposes, however, we can focus on two features of the forms which clearly worried Plato and were major butts of Aristotle's animadversions.

Aristotle held that if the forms were, as Plato said, entities that existed in their own right, they could never serve to implement the philosophical projects of definition and division (that is, classification into genera and species). This is just what Plato had discussed at length in the *Sophist:* the question of how the forms could blend or mix. Aristotle thought that blending or mixing were just what the forms could not do if they had the independent existence on which Plato insisted. Aristotle's objections seem to have depended, at least in part, on the assumption that each form was one and indivisible, and therefore could not be "subdivided" as was required by the method of division or by some ways of arriving at a definition.[7]

This objection to the forms is not apt to disturb us today. We are

7. See Harold Cherniss, *Aristotle's Criticism of Plato and the Academy* (Baltimore: Johns Hopkins University Press, 1944), chap. 1.

not bothered by the idea that the forms, although one, can have other forms "fall under" them. For us, this means no more than that the forms have logical relations. Thus anything that participates in the form Man must participate in the form Animal, that is, whatever has the property of being a man must have the property of being an animal. Logical relations among properties are nothing like the relation of part to whole in material objects, or like the relation between a property and the particulars that instantiate it. Material objects do not have logical relations, while properties do. This is a salient difference between properties and material objects and between names and predicates.

There is one criticism Aristotle leveled against the forms which, though wrongheaded, is worth serious attention, and that is Aristotle's rejection of the idea that the forms are totally separate from their instances. We are apt to discount this complaint on the grounds that Aristotle failed to appreciate the abstract character of the forms. This is apparent from the fact that Aristotle says the forms are too much like their instances, or just too much like material objects generally. It is true that some things Plato says about the forms invite this criticism, for example that the forms are superior to material objects in that they are unchanging. Aristotle scoffs at this ground for distinguishing the forms from material particulars, claiming that longevity may be a trait of some material particulars (e.g., stars). Again, if the forms are models for the particulars that instantiate them, they must share with particulars their size, shape, and so forth. These complaints may apply to the theory of forms of the *Republic* and other middle dialogues, but such difficulties are not clearly relevant to the treatment of the forms in the later dialogues (except, perhaps, in the *Timaeus*).

Aristotle again and again reverts to the claim that if the forms are to serve as universals, then they cannot be separate from the entities of which they are properties. Aristotle agrees with Plato that universals, like the forms, are the objects of scientific study, that they are changeless, and above all, that they exist. Where Aristotle differed from Plato was in holding that although universals are not identical with the things of which they are properties, they exist only by virtue of the existence of the things of which they are properties. If universals existed independently, they would take their place alongside the things that instantiate them. Separate existence is just what would make universals like other particulars and thus no longer universal.

But doesn't this argument show Aristotle to be confused? If universals can be talked about, they can be referred to. Yet whatever can be referred to is a particular. Confusion seems to have set in: universals are both particulars and at the same time necessarily distinct from particulars. Further, the fact that the existence of universals depends on the existence of the objects they characterize poses new problems that can be evaded only by counterintuitive measures. For there would seem to be properties that cannot be instantiated, for example, the property of being round and square, and there are properties that surely never will be instantiated, for example, the property of being a woman one hundred meters tall.

Given the difficulties, it may appear that Aristotle was more intent on emphasizing his differences with Plato than with maintaining a consistent, defensible thesis. But there are, of course, a number of reasons I have not mentioned in favor of Aristotle's position, and one of them is directly connected with the problem of predication. The point will become clearer if we turn to Aristotle's treatment of names and verbs.

In *De Interpretatione* Aristotle concentrates on sentences or statements which have a truth value, true or false (he holds that prayers and commands are neither true nor false). A sentence, he says, is a significant spoken sound some part of which is significant separately, that is, it must contain parts which are independently meaningful, though the parts alone cannot be used to affirm something. If a sentence or statement is to have a truth value or serve to make a statement, it must contain both a name and a verb. Aristotle apparently has Plato's solution of the problem of false statements in the *Sophist* in mind, where Plato claimed that every sentence must contain both a name and a verb. Thus Aristotle tells us that to speak a word such as 'man', 'runs', or 'wins' is not to make a statement or to say something true or false, but when such terms are combined in the right way an affirmation is produced. In the *Sophist* Plato had limited the discussion to names of human agents and verbs of action, but Aristotle explicitly broadens the scope of both names and verbs. Subject expressions for Aristotle include both common nouns like 'animal' and names like 'Philo'. In the *Categories* Aristotle provides a list of predicate types (κατηγορίαι). These comprise the category of substance (man, horse), of quantity (four cubits long), of quality (white, grammatical), of relation (double, half, larger), of location (in the Lyceum, in the agora), of time (yesterday, last year), of posture (lying down, sitting), of dress (shod, in armor), of action (cutting, burning), and of affection (being cut, being burned).

It is not altogether clear whether the predicate (or verb) includes what we express in English by the copula 'is' and its variants.[8] Aristotle says that 'health' is a name, but 'is healthy' is a verb. In Greek 'is healthy' is a single word (ὑγιαίνει). This would seem right, except that he also says verbs are names. Clearly verbs cannot be names in the same sense in which subject expressions are names without erasing the distinction between names and verbs on which Aristotle insists. Part of the point of saying that verbs are names may be that they are independently significant parts, as we say, of

8. According to Richard Patterson, in Aristotle, "a separate copula, where it does appear, functions to signify the affirmation or denial [when the copula is negated, 'is not'] of some predicate of a subject." *Aristotle's Modal Logic* (Cambridge: Cambridge University Press, 1995), p. 18. In other words, the copula connects the terms in a premise or conclusion of a syllogism. But then, is it the essential verb?

speech. But Aristotle has something more in mind. At the end of Chapter 3 of *De Interpretatione* he explains that when a verb is uttered by itself, or even with a copula, it does not necessarily entail the existence of a universal. It is only when the verb is predicated of something that exists that the verb signifies a universal. So verbs are not names in the same way subject expressions are; it is only if some substance instantiates the universal that the verb refers to something, that is, becomes a name. As Michael Frede puts it, "To understand this, it helps to remember that for both Plato and Aristotle, though in different ways, to say that Socrates is healthy is to attribute being both to Socrates and to health. After all, one sense or way in which health exists is that there are things which are healthy."[9]

Aristotle recognized that there was a deep difficulty involved in Plato's treatment of the forms as "separate" from the particulars which participate in them. If all we can say about the function of the forms in explaining the role of predicates is that predicates somehow bring the forms into the picture, then however we understand the relation of the predicate to a form, the sentence is reduced to bringing in, by naming, referring, or some other device, another entity. Surely a sentence knits these two entities together; otherwise the unity of the sentence is lost. How can a sentence be true or false if all it does is name or otherwise refer to two entities, Theaetetus and the form, Sitting or Flying? By insisting on the inseparability of object and universal, Aristotle invites us to see a single entity, Theaetetus flying or Theaetetus sitting. A sentence such as 'Theaetetus sits' affirms the existence both of Theaetetus and of the universal Sitting, but as a single entity, Theaetetus *with* the property of sitting. The sentence affirms the singleness, truly or falsely.

This may be, in part, the reason why Aristotle rejected Plato's in-

9. Michael Frede, "Aristotle on Nouns and Verbs in *De Interpretatione* 2–3," in *Aristotle's De Interpretatione,* ed. M. Frede and M. Mignucci (Oxford: Oxford University Press, forthcoming).

dependently existing forms. But it would be foolish to say that Aristotle has solved the problem of predication. Viewed simply as a metaphysical theory, it is not obvious that it is unsatisfactory. But even as metaphysics it ought to puzzle us. If the fact that Theaetetus is sitting consists in just a single entity, the seated Theaetetus, then what do we add by saying the universal *also* exists? Is the thought that properties exist prompted by such obvious facts as that people may be sitting or even, to skip a few thousand years, flying? If we turn to the semantic version of predication, it is easier to understand why Aristotle felt constrained to say the universal existed, though only in a way that made its existence depend on the existence of the substances that instantiated it. In explaining the complexity of even the simplest sentences, the complexity on which both Aristotle and Plato agreed, there must be, at a minimum, two separable elements, supplied by a name and a verb. The particularity of what the name refers to is completed by the generality introduced by the verb. That generality makes the verb capable of applying to endless other particulars. To explain this feature of the verb it seems necessary to introduce an entity, the universal.

The need to introduce an entity to explain the function of verbs or predicates has been assumed or postulated or argued for by most philosophers who have been interested in the structure of sentences and the thoughts that sentences can be used to express. Nevertheless, once this need is satisfied, a further problem arises, for the sentence does not just bring two entities into view; it also expresses the thought that the particular named by the name instantiates the property which provides the semantic content of the verb. What, in the sentence itself, expresses this thought? Aristotle seems at one point to suggest that the copula, written separately, or combined with the verb, tells us that the named entity, for instance Theaetetus, *is* an entity with a certain property. It is easy enough to sympathize with Aristotle's insistence that the copula itself brings in no new entity. We sympathize because if it did bring in a new entity, we would once more face the regress. But sympathy is one thing; clear understanding is another. What is impossible to understand is why, if the function of a verb is to introduce a universal, the copula, expressed or not, does not in turn introduce another universal, this time a relation that must be expressed in every sentence. Aristotle has not solved the problem of predication.

Let us give Aristotle full credit, though, for having recognized the problem, and having made an honorable attempt to restore unity to the sentence and the ontology that lies behind it. The thesis that universals exist only in the particulars they inform takes a step beyond Plato, for it introduces a difference between particulars and universals which emphasizes their different ontological roles and thus emphasizes the difference between subjects and predicates.

I do not intend to follow the history of theories of predication through the tens of centuries that separate us from Plato and Aristotle.[10] It is reasonable to ask why philosophers have not succeeded by now in solving this simple, though absolutely basic, problem. But the truth is that if they have, no one seems to know that they have. The next chapter surveys what a few more recent philosophers have said on the subject, and it will be apparent that they have made remarkably little progress. For the most part, though, contemporary philosophers have not even recognized that there is a problem. That is why I have dwelt on Plato and Aristotle, for their thinking led to the problem, and both seem to have been alive to the need to resolve it.

The problem arises, as we have seen, in the case of the simplest

10. [Charles Parsons comments: "Something of the overview Davidson asks for was given by Ernst Tugendhat in *Vorlesungen zur Einführung in der sprachanalytische Philosophie* (Frankfurt: Suhrkamp, 1976). Although that work has been translated into English (under the title *Traditional and Analytical Philosophy*), it hasn't gotten the attention it deserves in the English-speaking world. Davidson would probably find Tugendhat's positive view too close to Strawson's."]

sentences, like 'Theaetetus sits'. But this does not mean the problem is restricted to such cases. Aristotle gave examples of many other predicates that can be attached to a name—'is a man', 'is wearing armor', 'is in the agora', and so on—but he failed to provide a clear definition of the concept of a predicate, leaving it unclear whether the copula and other features of sentences should be considered part of the predicate. Aristotle's logic was not formalized, nor could it be formalized without a clearer sense of the syntactic structure and semantics of sentences. In particular, the treatment of expressions like 'all men', 'some man', and 'no man' as self-contained terms masked the essential nature of predicates, quantifiers, and the apparatus of cross-reference implemented in natural languages by pronouns. This is not a criticism of Aristotelian logic; many of the inferences it accepted are valid. It remains the case, however, that although Aristotle gave logic a brilliant start, his own logic resisted the inclusion of countless further forms of valid inference. The limitations inherent in syllogistic logic were not overcome until late in the nineteenth century.

In order to display the problem of predication more clearly, let me turn briefly to how modern logic and semantics view predicates. Plato and Aristotle were right that many verbs are predicates, and that every sentence that can be used to make an assertion must contain, at least implicitly, a verb. But the concept of a predicate has been vastly expanded. We now think of adjectives, like 'green', 'voluptuous', 'just', 'square', as parts of predicates, like 'is green', 'is square', 'is just'. Common nouns, such as 'man', 'animal', and 'skyscraper', we also treat as inseparable parts of predicates, such as 'is a man', 'is a skyscraper', and so on. The stock of predicates has grown larger and richer by admitting predicates that relate objects to one another. Thus 'is larger than' and 'is taller than' are admitted as two-place predicates, and further predicates express relations of any number of places. The notion of identity, which is expressed by a homonym of the copula 'is', just illustrated, is expressed by another two-place predicate: 'Truth is Beauty', 'Colin Powell is the present Secretary of State'.

The notion of "places" in a predicate is the key to the modern concept of a predicate. Any expression obtained from a sentence by deleting one or more singular terms from the sentence counts as a predicate; the spaces left in a predicate when singular terms are removed are the places. If we keep track of the positions from which singular terms have been subtracted by inserting 'x', 'y', 'z', and so forth in the vacated positions, then 'x loves y' is one predicate, 'John loves x' and 'x loves Susan' are others, and 'x loves x' still another. The truth functions for conjunction, negation, alternation, and so on also serve to help construct more complicated predicates such as 'x is tall and x is handsome and x is not wealthy'. Finally, there are the quantifiers 'all', 'every', 'each', and 'some' which bind variables that may occupy the places in predicates instead of singular terms.

This is not the whole story, of course. But the devices just informally described suffice to represent the underlying structure of a great number of the sentences in natural languages. Furthermore, when augmented by appropriate rules of inference, many of the inferences in natural languages that we accept are authorized, including all valid syllogistic inferences. There are plenty of unresolved questions about the exact relations between the syntax and logic of first-order quantification theory, which is what is adumbrated in the preceding paragraph, and the syntax and semantics of natural languages. I shall not be delving deeply into such questions here. The resources of quantificational languages and logic mirror the resources of natural languages well enough to justify treating the problem of predication as it applies in such cases. The problem in this form includes the problem as it came to life in the work of Plato and Aristotle. In its modern form, the problem is both clearer and more formidable—clearer because exactly what counts as a predicate is better defined, more formidable because of the infinity of structures that general quantification and the truth-functional connectives introduce. A full and satisfactory solution to the problem of predication will explain how predicates function in sentences to give sentences the unity demanded by the fact that sentences can be true or false and can be used to express judgments.

CHAPTER 5

Failed Attempts

David Hume writes, in an appendix to *A Treatise of Human Nature,* "If perceptions are distinct existences, they form a whole only by being connected together. But no connexions among distinct existences are ever discoverable by human understanding." Hume admitted that he could not discover any theory which gave him satisfaction on this subject. "In short," he wrote, "there are two principles, which I cannot render consistent; nor is it in my power to renounce either of them, viz. *that all our distinct perceptions are distinct existences,* and *that the mind never perceives any real connexion among distinct existences.*" He confesses that "this difficulty is too hard for my understanding . . . Others, perhaps, or myself, upon more mature reflexions, may discover some hypothesis, that will reconcile those contradictions."[1]

Although these remarks concern the problem of explaining the unity of the mind, it is clear that the difficulty also arises in connection with the unity of thoughts or judgments, which are components of the mind. Kant thought the fault lay in Hume's atomistic psychology. The principle of association, on which Hume depended, is passive according to Kant, while thought is "spontane-

1. David Hume, *A Treatise of Human Nature,* ed. L. A. Selby-Bigge (Oxford: Oxford University Press, 1951), pp. 635–636.

ous" and inherently purposeful. Concepts, Kant decreed, are predicates of possible judgments (*Critique of Pure Reason,* A69/B94). All acts of the understanding can be reduced to judgments, and every judgment involves a relation of representations. The active mind brings things together to form judgments.

The difficulty Hume found in explaining how impressions and ideas could be related except by association left him with the problem of explaining what sort of bundle a single mind is, and therefore what the medium might be in which association could take place. Exactly the same problem arises when we try to explain the unity of judgment, as Kant recognized. But while we may, or may not, think that Kant solved the problem of the unity of apperception, he said little that is relevant to the problem Plato and Aristotle wrestled with, the problem of predication. Kant classified the ways in which the mind puts elements together in judgment, but he does not seem to have recognized the importance of explaining exactly what the mind adds to the elements to produce a judgment. Kant realized that Hume had no way of accounting for the unity of a judgment, a fact that Hume in effect noticed. But, unlike Hume, Kant did not see that he had not addressed the problem of predication. In any case, Hume was not the only philosopher to confess that the unity of sentences or judgments was something he could not explain. Another such philosopher was Bertrand Russell.

Russell had the advantage of knowing modern logic. But this did not help him solve the problem of predication, a problem with which he struggled long and hard. Modern logic, with its recognition of relations and quantification, did, however, allow Russell to make the problematic nature of predication clearer. Leibniz, whom Russell greatly admired and about whom he wrote a book, held that "in every affirmative true proposition, necessary or contingent, universal or singular, the notion of the predicate is contained in some way in that of the subject, *praedicatum inest subjecto*. Or else

I do not know what truth is."[2] This was Leibniz's answer to the question of how a proposition becomes a unit: what it affirms or denies is the existence of a single entity with one or more attributes. Leibniz attributed his thesis to Aristotle, and we are certainly reminded of Aristotle's rejection of the Platonic view of the separate existence of the forms. But there is a difference: Aristotle held that universals, though they existed only as they inhered in particulars, were nevertheless entities in their own right; Leibniz was a nominalist who did not believe in the existence of properties. This may seem to have spared Leibniz the problem that faced Aristotle of explaining how particular and universal are related, but it hardly helped solve the semantic problem of how subject and predicate are related. Leibniz was as skeptical about the existence of relations as of properties. The rejection of relations took Leibniz to a Parmenidean extreme. Where Parmenides had concluded that there could exist just one monadic substance about which nothing true (much less false) could be said, Leibniz allowed for an infinity of monads, each completely self-sufficient, mirroring a world with which it had no relations.[3]

Russell and G. E. Moore, who accepted the existence of relations, reacted strongly against the idea that the unity of the proposition depends on human acts of judgment.[4] They reasoned, as did Kant's

2. From *Leibniz: Philosophical Writings*, ed. G. H. R. Parkinson, trans. Mary Morris and G. H. R. Parkinson (London: J. M. Dent, 1973), p. 62.

3. Russell remarks on these connections: being clear about the nature of subjects and predicates, he says, "is important, since the issues between monism and monadism, between idealism and empiricism, and between those who maintain and those who deny that all truth is concerned with what exists, all depend, in whole or in part, upon the theory we adopt in regard to the present question." Bertrand Russell, *Principles of Mathematics* (Cambridge: Cambridge University Press, 1903), p. 43.

4. For more on this topic, see Peter Hylton, "The Nature of the Proposition and the Revolt against Idealism," in *Philosophy in History*, ed. R. Rorty, J. Schneewind, and Q. Skinner (Cambridge: Cambridge University Press, 1984), pp. 375–397.

idealist followers, that this view suggests that reality itself depends on human experience and judgment. But Russell and Moore, unlike Kant's idealist followers, rejected the premise. Russell in particular decided that unless the unity of the proposition can be explained entirely in terms of the proposition itself, without appeal to acts of judgment, there can be no objective truth.

In *Principles of Mathematics,* which was first published in 1903, Russell takes propositions to be entities which exist quite apart from judgments, words, or sentences. "*Words*," he wrote in italics, "all have meaning, in the simple sense that they are symbols which stand for something other than themselves. But a proposition, unless it happens to be linguistic (i.e., to be about words), does not contain words: it contains the entities indicated by words."[5] The existence of propositions does not in general depend on the existence of minds or thought; propositions are aspects or parts of the world. Propositions are made up of combinations or complexes of parts, but not every complex of parts is a proposition; propositions have, so to speak, a syntax.[6]

Although Russell believed that the structure of a proposition is not necessarily the same as the grammatical structure of a sentence, the latter is *prima facie* evidence of the former. He writes:

> The correctness of our philosophical analysis of a proposition may . . . be usefully checked by the exercise of assigning the meaning of each word in the sentence expressing the proposition. On the whole, grammar seems to me to bring us much nearer to a correct logic than the current opinions of philosophers; and in what follows, grammar, though not our master, will yet be taken as our guide.[7]

5. Russell, *Principles of Mathematics,* p. 47.
6. Here, and in what follows, I am much indebted to Leonard Linsky, "The Unity of the Proposition," *Journal of the History of Philosophy* 30 (1992): 243–273.
7. Russell, *Principles of Mathematics,* p. 42.

Russell finds three parts of speech especially important: substantives, adjectives, and verbs. But it is their objective correlates that are the constituents of propositions, and he uses the same words to refer to the correlates as to the parts of speech. Applied to the structure of a proposition, grammar is definitely not the master. Thus the words 'human' and 'humanity' are grammatically adjective and substantive respectively, but according to Russell they "denote precisely the same concept,"[8] a concept being a term in a proposition. In the sentence 'Socrates is human' the name 'Socrates' names the person Socrates, who counts as a term in the proposition expressed by the sentence. Socrates, Russell says, is a thing, because Socrates can never occur otherwise than as a term: he cannot occur as an adjective or a verb (these last two here being parts of a proposition). In addition to Socrates (the man himself), the proposition that Socrates is human contains a verb (expressed by the word 'is') and an adjective (expressed by the word 'human'). The verb is a relation between the man and the concept. The sentence 'Humanity belongs to Socrates', though "equivalent" to 'Socrates is human', expresses a different proposition, because the proposition expressed by 'Humanity belongs to Socrates' is *about* the concept of humanity while the proposition expressed by 'Socrates is human' is not. In the case of the proposition expressed by 'Socrates is human', "the concept is used as a concept, that is, it is actually predicated of a term"; in the case of the proposition expressed by 'Humanity belongs to Socrates', "the concept is itself said to have a predicate," namely that of belonging to Socrates. Although Russell does not explain how a single concept can satisfy two such different roles, he recognizes that this is a troublesome issue. Russell distinguishes two sorts of concept, adjectives and verbs. The former are "often called predicates or class-concepts; the latter are always or almost always relations." This passage is immediately followed by a parenthetical remark:

8. Ibid.

"In intransitive verbs, the notion expressed by the verb is complex, and usually asserts a definite relation to an indefinite relatum, as in 'Smith breathes'."[9] In this sentence the word 'breathes' both introduces the concept of breathing and does the work of a copula, relating Smith and the concept.

Russell goes on to discuss the problem of understanding the difference between true and false propositions. There is a difficulty, which, he says, "seems to be inherent in the very nature of truth and falsity, [and] is one with which I do not know how to deal satisfactorily." The trouble is that propositions are entities, and Russell has maintained that any entity can be a logical subject. But if we say that some proposition is true or false, we are saying that an entity is true or false, which makes no sense. If we ask what is asserted in the proposition expressed by 'Caesar died', the answer seems to be 'the death of Caesar'. Yet the death of Caesar cannot be said to be true or false. Russell concludes, rather lamely, that there is a sense of assertion "very difficult to bring before the mind clearly, and yet quite undeniable, in which only true propositions are asserted."[10] The problem apparently arises if we take a sentence to express a *thing,* whether that thing is a proposition, a meaning, or anything else.[11]

The notion of the truth or falsity of an assertion, a proposition, or a sentence was puzzling enough for Russell, but there was another puzzle, this one central to his concerns, which he took even more seriously. It concerned the question of the unity of the proposition: how, Russell asked, does the verb unite the proposition? The puzzle arises in the case of the simplest propositions, such as that expressed by 'Socrates is human'. What is at issue is whether the verb here expresses a relation. If, as Russell claims, this proposition has only one term (Socrates), then the word 'is' cannot express a relation "in the ordinary sense . . . In fact, subject-predicate propo-

9. Ibid., p. 44.
10. Ibid., p. 49.
11. [Davidson wrote here: "Emphasize the comparison with Frege."]

sitions are distinguished by just this non-relational character. Nevertheless, a relation between Socrates and humanity is certainly *implied,* and it is very difficult to conceive the proposition as expressing no relation at all."[12] Again, it is the distinction between 'human' and 'humanity' which is making trouble. What is this difference, between a relation "in itself" and a relation as "actually relating"? Russell tries to explain in the following well-known, and rather astonishing, passage:

> Consider, for example, the proposition 'A differs from B.' The constituents of this proposition, if we analyze it, appear to be only A, difference, B. Yet these constituents, thus placed side by side, do not reconstitute the proposition. The difference which occurs in the proposition actually relates A and B, whereas the difference after analysis is a notion which has no connection with A and B. It may be said that we ought, in the analysis, to mention the relations which difference has to A and B, relations expressed by *is* and *from* when we say 'A is different from B.' These relations consist in the fact that A is referent and B relatum with respect to difference. But 'A, referent, difference, relatum, B' is still merely a list of terms, not a proposition. A Proposition, in fact, is essentially a unity, and when analysis has destroyed the unity, no enumeration of constituents will restore the proposition. The verb, when used as a verb, embodies the unity of the proposition, and is thus distinguishable from the verb considered as a term, though I do not know how to give a clear account of the precise nature of the distinction.[13]

Here Russell echoes Plato and Aristotle when they insisted that every sentence capable of being used to make an assertion must contain a verb. But there is one important difference: Russell did, while Plato and Aristotle did not, have the concept of a relation. Plato, as we have seen, spoke of the form Difference which related the forms

12. Russell, *Principles of Mathematics*, p. 49.
13. Ibid., pp. 49–50.

Motion and Rest, but the concept of a relation was never explicitly accepted as what a verb could express.

But Russell did not solve the problem of predication. When he tries to explain the role of the essential verb in a sentence, he analyzes the proposition the sentence expresses. But analysis finds that what corresponds to the verb in the sentence is just another term. Thus under analysis the proposition has lost its unity; it has become "merely a list of terms." If one thinks of the proposition as giving the semantics of the sentence it expresses, it is clear that Russell failed to explain the unity of either the sentence or the proposition. In spite of the confusion about the role of verbs, however, the character of the problem has become more sharply defined. The clarification is due to a better appreciation of the concept of a predicate; it is real progress to recognize that one-, two-, and more-place verbs are equally predicates, and that relations and properties must be treated in the same general way. The difficulty, for Russell as for Plato and Aristotle, was in reconciling the idea that verbs and predicates "stand for" or "indicate" entities (for Russell, constituents of propositions) with the need to preserve the unity of the statement or judgment or proposition expressed by a sentence, or the meaning of a sentence.

It is ironic that F. H. Bradley had formulated much the same problem in 1893.[14] He asked how a relation can really relate two (or more) things, for if the relation is, as he put it, "nothing to" the things related, "then they are not related at all. But if it is something to them, then clearly we now shall require a *new* connecting relation. For the relation hardly can be the mere adjective of one or both of its terms." In other words, there must be relations between the two things originally said to be related and the relation said to relate them, and so we are off on the familiar regress. Bradley con-

14. [Charles Parsons notes: F. H. Bradley, *Appearance and Reality* (London: S. Sonnenschein, and New York: Macmillan), 1897, is a second edition from the same publisher. Oxford is the publisher only of reprints published after Bradley's death.]

cluded that "this problem is insolvable. If you take the connection as a solid thing, you have got to show, and you cannot show, how the other solids are jointed to it. And, if you take it [the supposed relation] as a kind of medium or insubstantial atmosphere, it is a connection no longer." Relations are therefore "unintelligible."[15]

It is just this conclusion, not so different from Leibniz's or Parmenides' views of relations, that Russell had set out to refute. The irony of which I spoke is that the problem Bradley propounds in this passage is precisely the problem which Russell confessed left him without a solution. The difference is that Bradley held that the problem constituted a reductio of the thesis that there are such things as relations, while Russell continued to insist on the reality of relations despite the fact that he could not give a consistent account of the relations which unify a proposition. In this debate Bradley won, although Russell was on the right side.

Russell soon came to doubt his original theory of propositions. The reason was a difficulty which he had not recognized when he wrote *Principles*. Consider the proposition that Mars is identical with Venus. Mars and Venus are components of the proposition, and since the proposition is a unified entity, Mars and Venus must be actually related by the identity relation. If propositions are the objects of belief, which they must be if declarative sentences express propositions, then the objects of false beliefs must be as real as the objects of true beliefs. But there seems to be nothing in the propositions to explain this difference, for every constituent is equally real in both cases, including the verb that unites the proposition. But since propositions are the objective counterparts of beliefs and sentences, there is no explaining falsehood. The problem is analogous to the one raised by Parmenides and which Plato discussed in the *Sophist*.

By 1910 Russell had definitely given up his original theory and embraced a new one. According to this view, the entities that com-

15. Bradley, *Appearance and Reality*, p. 28.

pose what had been a proposition are all just listed; even the basic verb, typically a relation, is now passive, not operating as a verb that holds things together. If Carlos believes that Romeo loves Juliet, his belief or judgment is a real relation of Carlos to three entities: Romeo, the relation of loving, and Juliet. Since the relation of loving is not an active verb, it does not relate Romeo and Juliet. The active, and so unifying, relation exists only in Carlos's mind. Truth and falsehood can now be explained by saying that Carlos's belief, or the sentence that expresses it, is true if the active verb of loving relates Romeo and Juliet, otherwise false.

It is clear that what had been the proposition has disappeared from this analysis. What now has unity involves a thinking person: nothing is true or false aside from people, their thoughts, and their sentences. There is another complex unit, namely the loving of Juliet by Romeo, and Russell calls this a "fact." It is facts that make beliefs, judgments, and sentences true, when they are true. This is a straightforward correspondence theory: true beliefs, judgments, and sentences correspond to facts. Facts themselves are, of course, neither true nor false: they simply exist, and in general their existence has nothing to do with, and does not depend on, the existence of people, their thoughts, or their utterances. There is a clear statement of this theory in Russell's 1912 *Problems of Philosophy*.

Russell did not return to the question of the unity of the proposition, since on the new theory there were no propositions left. The new theory is clearly superior to the old in that it offers an account of truth. But the new theory is also puzzling in a way the old one was. It requires two united entities, the judgment and the fact (in the case of true judgments), and understanding what unites these complexes remains as difficult to explain as the unity of the proposition was. In this crucial matter, Russell has made no progress, for he has not explained how a verb can play the curious double role, sometimes picking out an object and sometimes being used *as* a verb.

I turn to the views of Peter Strawson, which in some ways are interestingly similar to Russell's. In a recent autobiographical sketch Strawson "describes and explains . . . a concern or preoccupation which has been central to a great part of [his] work—which has been, if you like, its *leit-motif*." This preoccupation is, he writes, "a concern with a certain fundamental operation of speech and thought and with the objects of that operation. The operation in question is that of identifying some *individual* item and characterizing or describing it in some *general* way; or, in other words, of definite singular reference together with predication."[16] The first question to be answered is this: what is it, in reality and in our thought about reality, that underlies and accounts for the formal distinction of the two types of term which enter into this basic combination? Strawson goes on to list some of the many places where he has tried to answer this question, including his book *Subject and Predicate in Logic and Grammar*.[17] He remarks that although his treatment of the issue differs from publication to publication, the various treatments are complementary rather than conflicting. "For central to all of them," he writes, "is the explicit thesis, or implicit assumption, that what at bottom sustains or underlies the formal distinction of terms in the fundamental combination is the ontological or metaphysical distinction between *spatio-temporal particulars* on the one hand and *general concepts or universals* on the other."[18] He is quick to point out that, as he puts it, his conclusion is perfectly standard; he claims originality only for his "explanatory arguments" for the conclusion.

One can only praise Strawson's ground-breaking discussions of the ways in which we identify and re-identify macroscopic physical

16. P. F. Strawson, "My Philosophy," in *The Philosophy of P. F. Strawson*, ed. P. K. Sen and R. R. Verma (New Delhi: Indian Council of Philosophical Research, 1995), pp. 1–18.

17. P. F. Strawson, *Subject and Predicate in Logic and Grammar* (London: Methuen, 1974).

18. Strawson, "My Philosophy," p. 9.

objects. Subject, or individual, terms are at their best when they name or otherwise pick out relatively enduring substantial spatio-temporal particulars like people or islands. But we frequently refer also to universals themselves and other abstract objects, treating them as subjects of predication, as when we say 'Courage is part of true virtue'. In cases like this, the notion of the object of reference can, Strawson tells us, take wings and mount into the sphere of the abstract, "so that the general or universal, the concept or idea, is no longer confined to its basic predicative role, but can figure *itself* as an object, a subject of its own predicates. So it appears; and so, I think, it is. There is . . . nothing wrong or metaphysically question-able in this appearance."[19] Strawson resists the idea that we speak this way only because it is convenient, given that we can rephrase the sentence 'Courage is a necessary part of true virtue' as 'No man is truly virtuous unless he is courageous', where there is "no appar-ent reference to the thing *courage*." He goes on to criticize Quine's nominalistic attitude toward universals, though he recognizes that Quine accepts the existence of classes, which are equally abstract objects. Strawson has no difficulty with Quine's Fregean slogan "No entity without identity" as long as it is "sufficiently generously treated," and he argues that if the slogan is so treated, we will find no difficulty in treating universals as existing entities. We don't need strict principles of individuation for universals, Strawson argues, because they *are* such principles.[20]

Quine made something like this last point in *Word and Object.* There Quine remarks that certain terms, like 'man', "possess built-in modes, however arbitrary, of dividing their reference." Quine then goes on to describe predication:

> The basic combination in which general and singular terms find their contrasting roles is that of *predication:* 'Mama is a woman,' or sche-

19. Ibid., p. 11.
20. Ibid., pp. 11, 12.

matically '*a* is an *F*' where '*a*' represents a singular term and '*F*' a general term. Predication joins a general term and a singular term to form a sentence that is true or false according as the general term is true or false of the object, if any, to which the singular term refers.[21]

Strawson strongly criticized this description of predication and the surrounding text which further characterized singular and general terms.[22] Strawson finds the description of what Quine calls the "contrasting roles" of singular and general terms not so much wrong as failing to provide anything more than a grammatical criterion for the distinction, with no explanation of why there should be such a distinction. Quine's account, Strawson says, "contains no attempt to mention any contrast there may be *in role or function*" between the two sorts of term.[23] Quine speaks of singular terms as *referring* to objects (or at least purporting to refer to objects), while general terms are *true of* any number of objects from zero on up. Strawson complains, however, that the difference marked by these semantical phrases is not really explained. Strawson fails to mention that in other sections of *Word and Object* and elsewhere Quine has said a good deal about these matters, including the remark I quoted earlier about *divided* reference. It is true that in the passage just quoted Quine does not provide a full account of what Strawson considers the central function of singular terms, namely that of "*identifying* an object, of bringing it about that the hearer . . . knows *which* or *what* object is in question,"[24] and it is this function of names that Strawson rightly holds to be exemplary. In book after book Quine has emphasized the obvious fact that spatio-temporal

21. W. V. Quine, *Word and Object* (Cambridge, Mass.: MIT Press, 1960), p. 96.

22. P. F. Strawson, "Singular Terms and Predication," *Journal of Philosophy* 58 (1961): 393–412. Reprinted in P. F. Strawson, *Logico-Linguistic Papers* (London: Methuen, 1971), pp. 53–74.

23. Ibid., p. 68.

24. Ibid., p. 59.

objects are the objects we join with others in discriminating, caring about, and referring to, but he does not have the same interest in proper names; Quine is more concerned with the epistemological aspects of reference to easily ostended objects and aspects of the world. In any event, there is a more important difference between Strawson's and Quine's accounts of predication.

Before I come to this feature of Strawson's treatment of predication, it is worth noting that it is not only Quine whose treatment of predication Strawson finds inadequate. Strawson is also critical of Russell's theory of descriptions as an account "of the working of one class of definite singular terms, viz. singular descriptions."[25] According to Strawson, Russell's analysis completely suppresses the identificatory function of singular terms, for it substitutes for a definite description an explicit assertion to the effect that there exists just one thing with a certain property, and to do this is to do something quite different from identifying that thing for a hearer. At this point it would be useful to distinguish, as Quine and Russell do but Strawson does not, between the grammatical or logical function of singular terms and their *use* in specific, though common, situations.

Strawson is also unhappy with Peter Geach and Elizabeth Anscombe, both of whom in separate places have said that a mark of the difference between singular terms and predicates is that a predicate can be negated while a singular term cannot.[26] There is no denying that this is a legitimate distinction, but Strawson complains that neither Anscombe nor Geach has explained why there should be such a distinction. Strawson remarks that negation is just a special case of the more general fact that predicates can be complex (or,

25. Ibid., p. 63.
26. P. F. Strawson, "The Asymmetry of Subjects and Predicates," in *Language, Belief, and Metaphysics,* ed. H. E. Kiefer and M. K. Munitz (New York: State University of New York Press, 1970), pp. 96–115. References are to the reprint in Strawson, *Logico-Linguistic Papers.*

in his word, "compound"), and more general yet is the fact that predicates can express contradictory propositions when appended to the same singular term. The essential point is that predicates are logically related to other predicates; names have no logical relations.

To return to the basic difference between Strawson's and Quine's account of predication, a difference which was apparently lost on Strawson: It is what lies behind, and is the reason for, Quine's characterization of predicates as *true of* particulars. Strawson sees this as just another instance of Quine's policy of avoiding commitment to abstract entities when he can. It is true that Quine abjures *intensional* entities such as properties and relations on the grounds that their identity conditions are obscure. But Strawson misses the real point, which is that Quine sees no reason to suppose that predicates correspond to single entities *of any kind.*

Strawson does not sympathize with what he sees as Quine's ontological abstemiousness. Like so many other philosophers, Strawson holds that predicates designate objects, that is, attributes, universals, forms, ideas, properties, and relations. According to Strawson, in the sentences 'Sally is pretty' and 'Betty is witty' the words 'pretty' and 'witty' designate attributes. Quine had insisted that if these words designated entities, it should be possible to quantify into the positions occupied by the words by substituting variables for the terms 'pretty' and 'witty' and binding the variables with quantifiers. We should be able to say, 'For some *attribute x,* Sally has *x.*' Strawson responds that we do indeed say such things. He illustrates:

> Prettiness is a quality desirable in a date and Betty has prettiness and Sally has prettiness. Similarly with willingness. Wit is a quality desirable in a date and Betty has wit and Sally has not. Everything which Sally has and which is a quality desirable in a date is something Betty

has; but there is something which is a quality desirable in a date and which Betty has, which Sally does not have.[27]

Strawson recognizes that the word 'prettiness' is a substantive while the word 'pretty' is, or is part of, a predicate. But this grammatical distinction he holds to be superficial, and he mounts an argument to show that 'pretty' is "implicitly referential." The sentence 'Sally is pretty' is equally *about* Sally and prettiness: the name 'Sally' identifies the person the sentence is about, while the word 'pretty' identifies an attribute Sally has. Quine makes too much, Strawson thinks, of the difference between the substantive 'prettiness' and the predicate 'pretty'. Or is the predicate 'is pretty'? Strawson seems to ignore the difference, and we can see why. Strawson has run up against the problem of predication.

In the sentence 'Sally is pretty' we are told that the first and third words designate entities, and that that is their entire semantic function. Strawson has written at length about the character of the designated entities, one singular and the other general or universal. Still, if the word 'is' is doing no work, the sentence consists of just two designating words. If the 'is' is part of a semantically unstructured predicate, the problem remains the same, since all predicates, according to Strawson, designate universals. But if the 'is' expresses a relation between Sally and prettiness, we have only made the problem worse, assuming, as Strawson does, that relational predicates designate relations. Following Strawson's strategy turns 'Sally is pretty' into a triple of designators.

It is interesting that someone who made it "central" to his life's work to explain "singular reference together with predication" should, so far as I know, have paid no serious attention to what I am calling the problem of predication. This is particularly curious because Russell conspicuously sought a solution only to confess

27. Strawson, "Singular Terms and Predication," p. 66.

that he found the problem beyond him. Quine, alone among those I have discussed, escapes the usual regress by simply denying that predicates indicate, refer to, or are to be explained by their association with some single entity, such as a property, quality, universal, or attribute. Quine relates predicates to the things of which they can be predicated—hence his phrase 'true of': predicates are *true of* each and every thing (or pair or triple, etc., of things) of which the predicate can be truly predicated. This cannot be called a full account of the role of predicates. Its merit is negative: it does not invite a regress.

A philosopher who has taken the problem of predication seriously, and who is fully aware of the difficulties into which Russell, Strawson, and many others fell, is Wilfrid Sellars. His failure to explain predication is therefore different from the attempts we have examined. He approves of Quine for having insisted that predicates do not name, stand for, or otherwise depend on the existence of abstract entities like properties, relations, or even sets. Perhaps such entities exist, Sellars holds, but they do not serve to explain the semantic role of predicates or the fact that we can truly speak and think variously about them. Predicates like 'is red' (a one-place predicate), 'loves' (a two-place predicate), and 'between' (a three-place predicate) are not to be confused with the singular terms 'redness', 'the relation of loving', and 'betweenness'. So far, Sellars and Quine are in agreement. But Sellars goes further than Quine. He objects to Quine's way of distinguishing predicates when Quine says their positions in sentences are not positions into which we can quantify, for this does not advance our understanding of the essential role of predicates in sentences.

Sellars knows that Wittgenstein somehow persuaded Russell to give up his early theory of predication. That theory was not so much about sentences as about propositions, but since there was a correspondence between sentences and propositions, we can follow Sellars by treating Russell's theory as a semantical theory about words and sentences. Sellars thinks Russell came to understand that it will not solve the problem of predication (or account for the unity of the proposition) to take predicates as corresponding to properties and relations, because then it will be necessary to relate the property or relation to the things singular terms refer to. This, as is now obvious, leads at once to Bradley's argument that we will never finish the job of providing appropriate relations. At first Russell thought he could address the problem by distinguishing between predicates that just named properties or relations and properties or relations used as verbs. But this was just the distinction which Russell found he could not explain. Russell then apparently gave up trying to unify the sentence itself, and lodged the unity in a relation between the judge and the various things named in the sentence. To do this was, Sellars thought, to miss Wittgenstein's point. It is unclear, however, how Russell could have failed to grasp Wittgenstein's argument, since Russell gives a fairly straightforward account of this aspect of the *Tractatus* in the introduction to that book. It seems more likely that Russell understood Wittgenstein fairly well, but he was not persuaded that Wittgenstein's intuitions could be worked out in a satisfactory way; certainly no theory of predication put forward by Russell in his published work demonstrates that he ever endorsed anything like the theory he attributes to Wittgenstein in his introduction.

Here is how Sellars develops his Wittgenstein-inspired view. Suppose for a moment that we add a special symbol to every simple sentence which expresses the idea that the property named is a property of the named subject: perhaps the symbol is the word 'exemplifies'. Thus we will take the sentence 'Theaetetus sits' as naming Theaetetus and the property of sitting and also containing the special symbol 'exemplifies', so that the whole sentence means that Theaetetus is sitting. We will treat sentences which relate two or more things in roughly the same way, always adding the word 'exemplifies'. But since *every* sentence in these forms will contain this special word, we may as well leave it out (as, we are told, Arabic sometimes does). For that matter, we may as well revert to the original spelling, as long as we understand that the sentence 'Theaetetus sits' expresses the fact that Theaetetus exemplifies the property of sitting. But wait. If the notion of expressing something that can have a truth value is accomplished by the now unwritten symbol 'exemplifies', why not say that uniting the sentence is simply accomplished by the predicate itself? The predicate allows us to say something about one entity, perhaps Theaetetus. No second entity is required. If we understand the role which the symbol 'exemplifies' was invented to play and that role requires no extra entity, then we understand the role of a predicate without further props.

But Sellars says we *still* have not seen to the bottom of what Wittgenstein has to teach us. This is that even the predicate itself is dispensable. Thus, instead of writing 'Theaetetus sits' we could write just the name 'Theaetetus' in a way that expresses the fact that Theaetetus is sitting, perhaps by writing the name in a shape that pictures a man sitting. We are to imagine a different mode of name-shape for every non-complex predicate. Negations might be expressed by writing shaped names upside down. Sellars also thinks that we might express what we now express by the sentence 'a is larger than b' by writing the letter 'a' above the letter 'b'. The deep insight, he says, is that "we can *only* say that a is larger than b by placing the names 'a' and 'b' in a (conventional) dyadic relation."[28] The conventional relation is expressed by the way the names are related to each other in writing or in speech. We can change the convention at will: we can write 'a and b exemplify the relation of larger than', or we can omit the words 'exemplify the relation of' by writing 'a, b, larger than' or we can write 'a is larger than b' or we can write 'a' above 'b'. In each case, typography does the work of predication to produce a sentence which says that a is larger than b.

28. Wilfrid Sellars, *Naturalism and Ontology* (Atascadero, Calif.: Ridgeview, 1981), p. 50.

Sellars's emphasis on the fact that in a sentence the singular terms are displayed in a way that literally shows the meaning of a sentence is, of course, reminiscent of Wittgenstein's early picture theory of meaning: in one way or another, sentences represent aspects of the world by picturing them. Sellars does not endorse the picture theory, but he believes that we can, so to speak, learn from it what we need to understand without trying to develop the detailed geometry of picturing. What we should learn is that the usual assumption about predicates is false. Predicates do not, as names do, *stand in distinct and autonomous relations to extra-linguistic reality.*[29] Predicates have a legitimate role in sentences, but no autonomous role. To say something true or false about one or more objects, we write (or speak) the names in one of many possible conventional ways. The conventions let us know what is being said, period. According to Sellars, it follows that Quine is wrong when he says that predicates are true of objects or ordered n-tuples of objects, since this would be to put predicates into "distinct and autonomous relations to extra-linguistic reality."

We have run through a sequence of semantic and metaphysical or ontological theories about predicates and predication. The most common view is that predicates stand for (or are otherwise related to) abstract objects, properties, characteristics, qualities, relations, or sets. Some philosophers (for example, Aristotle, Frege, and Russell) have tried to avoid the full force, and so the consequences, of this idea, though not, to my mind, satisfactorily. Now we have Sellars's neo-Wittgensteinian thesis that predicates have no independently specifiable function, and thus have no independent semantic relation to the world. Can Sellars be right?

First we must ask what he means by "distinct and autonomous relations." Quine would certainly agree with Frege's dictum that it is only in the context of a sentence that any word has a meaning.

29. Wilfrid Sellars, "Towards a Theory of Predication," in *How Things Are*, ed. J. Bogen and J. E. McGuire (Dordrecht: Reidel, 1985), pp. 285–322; p. 314. Italics in the original.

Taken in this way, the claim that predicates are not autonomous is something we can say (when adequately protected) about any expression that is not a sentence. Sellars intends, however, to be saying something about predicates that is not true, for instance, of names or other singular terms, which do (usually) have an independently specifiable relation to extra-linguistic entities. Once more, Quine agrees: he has put the point by insisting that predicates are "syncategorematic," while singular terms are not.[30] But it does not follow that we cannot say what the roles of predicates are in the context of sentences. That has been one way of putting the problem of predication from the start. Quine would also agree that predicates do not name abstract objects or any other sort of objects, and he would go along with Sellars in rejecting Frege's idea that predicates refer to strange, incomplete non-objects. The disagreement apparently comes down, then, to Sellars's rejection of Quine's view that predicates (in sentences, of course) are true of objects.

It is by no means easy to see how Sellars's explanation of the truth of a simple sentence like 'Theaetetus sits' evades the necessity of taking the predicate 'sits' to be true of objects that are sitting. Here, much simplified, but not, I think, misrepresented, is Sellars's account. 'Theaetetus sits' should be viewed, quite literally, as a *way* of referring to Theaetetus; the usual way is given by spelling Theaetetus's name as 'Theaetetus' concatenated with the word 'sits'. Thus the name "has a character by virtue of which it belongs to a class of linguistic representatives of [seated] things."[31] This certainly seems to explain the role of the word 'sits' by reference to a class, the class of seated objects, but it does make a gesture in the direction of making the only direct reference in the sentence a reference to Theaetetus. In almost every other respect, however, Sellars's

30. For an excellent defense of this aspect of Quine's view of predicates, see Cora Diamond, *The Realistic Spirit* (Cambridge, Mass.: MIT Press, 1991), pp. 108–111.
31. Sellars, "Towards a Theory of Predication," p. 320.

suggestion seems impossible to work out. He does not say how complex predicates and quantification are to be treated, or how an account of truth can be given, without assigning a clear role to predicates.

One sympathizes with Sellars, because each of the steps he takes in retreat from the idea that predicates stand for abstract entities is appealing. But the outcome does not need to be that we cannot explain the role of predicates in sentences by relating them somehow to objects of the sorts the singular terms of the sentence refer to. Quine would have applauded Sellars's attempt to explain truth by reference to a set; this would be a great improvement on referring to a property, since classes have clear identity conditions, while properties do not. But Quine's view that predicates are true of objects is better, for it avoids reference to an abstract entity, a class, or anything else. The question remains, however, whether Quine's negative hint can be developed into a satisfactory way of explaining or describing the role of predicates.

CHAPTER 6

Truth and Predication

Theories of truth and theories of predication are closely related: it seems probable that any comprehensive theory of truth will include a theory of predication. We have already noted that Plato explained how it was possible to say or think what is false, as well as what is true, by appeal to a theory of predication; and Bertrand Russell's early account of predication made it impossible to explain truth, even for the simplest sentences—and for that reason, perhaps among others, Russell abandoned that account.

One reason for holding predication hostage to a theory of truth is that having a truth value is the simplest and clearest mark of the unity of sentences and of the beliefs and judgments that sentences can be used to express. For it is only an expression, the semantics of which demonstrate a clear relevance to truth values, that has the unique unity of a sentence. The claim of uniqueness can certainly be disputed. There are those who hold that it is possible to have a unified theory of the meaning of sentences without the need for an account of truth; some of these positions will be discussed presently. And there are many philosophers who maintain that sentences of one sort or another are neither true nor false.

What is the connection between truth and belief, which is all that the unified theory yields? The answer lies in the relation between belief and truth. Roughly, the idea is that we learn our first language (and subsequent ones if they are learned in context and not by using dictionaries or appealing to bilinguals) by assuming (not consciously) that others are mostly saying what they believe, and in basic cases what they believe is mostly true. This is not to say that truth is a norm. Ostension doesn't establish a norm; it simply creates a disposition, given our sense organs, and so on, that is, a conditioning of sentences to aspects of the world.[1] Of course, the learner may not "go on" as the others do. She will learn. But so much that is basic is built in.

There are many views of the nature of truth, and the choice among them is naturally related to how predication is explained and vice versa. Consider the question of what the proper bearers of truth and falsity are. Utterances and written tokens of sentences, insofar as they are the intentional products of thinking creatures, are typically true or false. Such tokens are objects or events in the material world. Are there other material entities that have a truth value? It seems not, as long we take utterances to include silent signing and other forms of coded signaling. There are abstract objects that we call true or false, particularly sentences when appropriately relativized to speakers, times, and circumstances. One good way to think of sentences themselves is as shapes, whether verbal, written, or otherwise signed. (Think, as Wittgenstein suggested, of what is common to the performance of a piece of music, a written score, and a recording of a performance of the piece.) We would have no special interest in these shapes if we did not think of them as sometimes instantiated with communicative intent and the instances understood by an audience. Nevertheless, we need these abstract entities if we want to theorize. We cannot say much in a theoretical vein about linguistic communication without talking of words and sentences. Names and predicates are likewise usually treated as ab-

1. [Davidson had added here that he should explain how ostension works. He said this much: "It works in practice even when there is plenty of joking, pretending, and so on."]

stract entities, though we may also call instances of these types names and predicates. The abstract entities—words and expressions built from words—are indispensable when we want to describe the syntax, semantics, and logical relations of the instances.[2]

These reflections remind us that the discussion of predication, and disagreements about it, must in the end be brought back to the worldly phenomena that prompted our interest in the first place. Still, we should head back to earth at the right time. We use language, as Wittgenstein and J. L. Austin emphasized, in endless ways, not only to make assertions but just as often to amuse, deceive, win fame, make promises, enter into contracts, give orders, ask questions, marry, or divorce. All of these activities are arguably sentential in nature, and so involve predication. What we count as linguistic performances are performed by uttering or inscribing expressions that are, in context, sentential.

How does truth fare in this motley collection? It is a mistake to suppose that the truth value of an utterance depends on whether the speaker or the speaker's hearers are concerned with the question of truth. If I now say, by way of example, 'It is snowing in Fairbanks, Alaska,' I do not care whether it is true, nor, I suspect, do you. Nevertheless, it *is* true. Or false, as the case may be. Many of the sentences spoken by an actor or a politician or written in a novel are true or false, but for the most part no one cares whether they are true. If you say to a visitor, "We just had this carpet cleaned, so we take off our shoes," what we say may be false, but we may hope our saying this will make it true; or perhaps the remark is meant as a

2. There are quibbles about whether it is really sentences or their tokens that are properly called truth-bearers. Among the candidates are propositions or "what is said" in uttering a sentence. There is no harm (or gain in my opinion) in such views as long as their proponents will generously allow me to carry on as if the truth or falsity of propositions or things said has been extended to the sentences and utterances of sentences that express the propositions or are the instruments of saying.

joke. In the case of metaphors, the sentences that contain them are typically obviously false or trivially true, because these are typically indications that something is intended as a metaphor. In such cases we need to know the literal meaning but are uninterested in the question of literal truth. The truth value of the plainest assertion may matter if someone is seriously misled or usefully warned, but there is no *linguistic* norm that decrees that we are misusing words if we lie, and certainly no linguistic norm to the effect that we should assert only what is true. What we do in making an assertion is represent ourselves as believing what we say, and so we may be morally at fault if it turns out that we don't believe what we asserted. But moral error is not linguistic error. Assertion, like issuing an order or asking a question, is a *force* we give to some utterances, and an utterance has a certain force only if the speaker intends his or her audience to be aware of the force and so of the intention. There are no linguistic conventions or rules which determine the force of an utterance, and so no regular relation between force and the literal truth or meaning of what is said. We cannot learn what sets apart utterances that aim at literal truth by the study of their force.

The connection, then, between speech acts of many kinds and concern with the truth value of what is said is extremely complicated, and does not lend itself easily to generalizations connecting such concern with the literal meaning of the sentences uttered. Meaning depends on use, but it is not easy to say how, for uses to which we may put the utterance of a sentence are endless while its meaning remains fixed. What does matter to understanding is the truth conditions of utterances, for if we do not know under what conditions an utterance would be true, we do not understand it. Whatever purposes a speaker hopes to promote by using language, we cannot fail to be interested in the truth conditions of the speaker's utterances as long as we are interested in what the speaker means by his words.

This brings us back to our subject, for the truth conditions of any sentence capable of truth or falsity depend, among other things, on the semantic function of one or more predicates. This may understate the role of predication, for sentences which many philosophers do not count as having a truth value certainly contain predicates. Imperatives, interrogatives, sentences which tell us our duties, or what is good, bad, or beautiful, all contain predicates. Some sentences of these types may be neither true nor false, but all of them are related logically or evidentially to sentences that are true or false, and it is unlikely that the semantics of such sentences can be given without appeal to their relations to sentences for which we know the truth conditions. This is obvious in the case of imperatives and interrogatives. We understand an imperative if and only if we know under what conditions what it orders or commands is obeyed. The possible answers to a question are sentences related syntactically and semantically to the question, and the answers have a truth value, even if the questions do not. Sentences which can be used to express values normally do so because they contain evaluative predicates, and we often assert such sentences with all the affirmative or negative force with which we utter sentences we believe to be true or false. In any case, the semantics of such sentences are a mystery if we do not think they have truth values. Truth and predication go together; no sentence is without a predicate, and most sentences, if not all, are understood only if their truth conditions, or the truth conditions of closely related sentences, are known.

But what is it for an utterance to be true? Many thinkers have turned to one form or another of correspondence as the key to truth. It will ease discussion if we think of sentences as the entities to which we will assign truth, even though their truth is inherited from utterances of sentences under appropriate circumstances. In other words, I plan for the time being to forget the necessary parameters like time and speaker. This simplification is warranted provided we believe we can accommodate the parameters when it matters. The problem concerns the entities correspondence to which is supposed to confer truth. The typical choice has been facts, sometimes called states of affairs, situations, or truth-makers. Russell, we remember, had at first taken sentences to express what he described as propositions, which were built from the objective counterparts of singular terms, quantifiers, and predicates (including relational predicates). Since these semantic counterparts of words were conceived as entities in, or features of, the world independent of thought, Russell often treated propositions as facts. What Russell discovered is that when propositions were treated in this way, correspondence became useless for explaining truth, since every meaningful sentence, true or false, expresses a proposition. Thus if correspondence to a proposition makes a sentence true, every sentence is true. This result is clearly absurd, since both a sentence and its negation would be true. When this consequence of his theory became clear to Russell, he gave up the theory. His subsequent theory distinguished between the meaning of a thought or judgment and the circumstances that make the thought or judgment true, and thus may be considered a sort of correspondence theory, though an unsatisfactory one. The difficulty springs from Russell's failure to give an adequate account of the unity either of the judgment or of what it is that makes it true, and this is the familiar failure to explain the simplest cases of predication. Judgments, on Russell's second theory, were united by the mind of the judge, while the fact judged was held together by a relation operating *as* a relation and not as an abstract object. The unifying element remained as mysterious as ever.

Quite apart from worries about predication, many philosophers cling to the idea that true sentences correspond to facts which are objective entities in the world, independent, for the most part, of thought. Such thinkers would be right not to be worried if the truth of sentences could be shown to depend on clearly individuated facts, for such dependence might suffice to account for the unity of sentences. The trouble with this course is that no one knows how to individuate facts in a plausible way.

One should be careful not to confuse the idea that true sentences (or the judgments or beliefs they can be used to express) correspond to clearly individuated facts with the idea that sentences are true or false because of "the way things are." To insist on the latter idea is to insist on no more than the objectivity of truth. Of course what we *believe* to be true is affected by many factors, and the concepts at our disposal define the range of thoughts and beliefs available to us. Our descriptions of the world are thus doubly dependent on us and on our circumstances. Nevertheless, our descriptions of the world are objectively true or false. Serious correspondence theories go beyond these platitudes and attempt to explain or characterize truth by invoking special entities to which complete sentences, if true, correspond.

Facts must be entities that exist objectively to serve this explanatory purpose. But what, exactly, are they? It is of no help, in answer to the question "What is the fact that makes the sentence 'Theaetetus sits' true?" to reply "The fact that Theaetetus sits." This tells us no more than that the sentence 'Theaetetus sits' is true if and only if Theaetetus sits, and while this is certainly right, its correctness does not involve an entity called a fact. 'It is a fact that Theaetetus sits' is just a wordy way of saying that Theaetetus sits. If we try to be more precise about the nature of facts, it is natural to start with the hunch that it is facts that true sentences purport to be "about." Thus 'Theaetetus sits' is certainly about Theaetetus. But we cannot suppose that Theaetetus himself is a fact, and therefore we cannot suppose that, even if he is seated, the seated Theaetetus is a fact. Once more we are reminded of Aristotle's attempt to rescue the unity of the sentence from Plato's dualistic universe by saying that the universal exists only in the particulars that instantiate it. But Aristotle was no correspondence theorist. Aristotle characterized truth, as we know, this way: *To say of what is that it is not, or of what is not that it is, is false, while to say of what is that it is, or of what is not that it is not, is true.* This formulation postulates no entities like facts. The things of which we say that they are or are not are the entities adverted to by the referring parts of sentences, not by sentences as wholes.

There is another, more basic, problem with appeal to facts to explain truth. In a review of Carnap's *Introduction to Semantics,* Alonzo Church credits Frege with an argument to show that if sentences correspond to whatever in the world makes them true, then all true sentences must correspond to the same thing.[3] Similarly, all false sentences must correspond to the same thing (though not, of course, the same thing that true sentences correspond to). Church put the basic argument into somewhat awkward English as follows:

> The denotation (in English) of 'Sir Walter Scott is the author of *Waverley*' must be the same as that of 'Sir Walter Scott is Sir Walter Scott,' the name 'the author of *Waverley*' being replaced by another which has the same denotation. Again, the sentence 'Sir Walter Scott is the author of *Waverley*' must have the same denotation as the sentence 'Sir Walter Scott is the man who wrote twenty-nine Waverley novels altogether,' since the name 'the author of *Waverley*' is replaced by another name of the same person; the latter sentence, it is plausible to suppose, [has the same denotation as] 'The number, such that Sir Walter Scott is the man who wrote that many Waverley novels altogether, is twenty-nine' . . . and from this last sentence in turn, replacing the complete subject by another of the same number, we obtain, as still having the same denotation, the sentence, 'The number of counties in Utah is twenty-nine.'[4]

3. Alonzo Church, "Carnap's *Introduction to Semantics*," *Philosophical Review,* 52 (1943): 298–304.

4. Alonzo Church, *Introduction to Mathematical Logic,* vol. 1 (Princeton: Princeton University Press, 1956), pp. 24–25.

The argument has thus shown that the two sentences, 'Sir Walter Scott is the author of *Waverley*' and 'The number of counties in Utah is twenty-nine', denote the same thing even though they have nothing significant in common except their truth value. In this passage Church speaks of sentences as *denoting* entities, but the argument applies equally if one thinks of sentences *naming* or *corresponding to* entities. The assumptions of the argument seem simple: if two sentences are logically equivalent, they correspond to the same thing, and what a sentence corresponds to is not changed if a singular term is replaced by a coreferring singular term.

This argument depends on the assumption that definite descriptions are singular terms and so may be substituted one for another without altering what a sentence corresponds to. Gödel, in his contribution to the Library of Living Philosophers volume on Russell,[5] thinks that Russell may have proposed his theory of definite descriptions with Frege's argument in mind. Russell realized that if definite descriptions are singular terms like names, as they seem to be, and we hold that sentences correspond to or designate propositions or facts, then the two sentences 'Scott is the author of *Waverley*' and 'Scott is Scott' would correspond to the same proposition or fact; this is one of the problems Russell emphasized when he made the case for his theory of definite descriptions. What Gödel points out is that it is the stronger conclusion, that all sentences with the same truth value correspond to the same fact, which may have led Russell to argue that definite descriptions are not singular terms but are syncategorematic expressions which disappear when the logical form of the sentences in which they appear is revealed.

Gödel's version of the argument is not the same as Church's, since it depends only on the nature of definite descriptions, while

5. Kurt Gödel, "Russell's Mathematical Logic," in *The Philosophy of Bertrand Russell,* ed. P. A. Schilpp (Evanston, Ill.: Northwestern University Press, 1944), pp. 128–129. I learned this from Stephen Neale's "The Philosophical Significance of Gödel's Slingshot," *Mind* 104 (1995): 761–825.

Church's calls on the resources of set theory. It is a bit surprising that neither Frege nor Russell ever, so far as I know, explicitly states the argument in either form. Dummett, however, and independently of Church, finds something like Gödel's argument to be clearly implicit in Frege's writings. Stephen Neale has tracked down much of what I am saying here about what has come to be known as the Slingshot argument (the term covers both Church's and Gödel's versions).[6] But Neale has done much more: he has set out the arguments in detail, and demonstrated the consequences. He shows that Gödel's argument is the more powerful, because it assumes less. And he concludes that although the postulation of facts has not been proven to be disastrous no matter what assumptions are made, the cost of the postulation is so high that it is unlikely to be deemed acceptable. So the Slingshot, though nowhere near as simple as I, or apparently Church, had thought, still leads to the same conclusion: the postulation of facts will not explain, define, or even illuminate the concept of truth. Gödel concludes his discussion of the logic implicit in Russell's rejection of facts with the words "I cannot help feeling that the problem raised by Frege's puzzling conclusion (that there is one fact at most) has only been evaded by Russell's theory of descriptions, and that there is something behind it which is not yet completely understood."[7] Neale has done much to make explicit what the evasion amounts to.

The Slingshot is not just an argument against facts as the entities correspondence to which one might have hoped would help explain truth. It is equally an argument against any entities that might be proposed as correspondents, say states of affairs or situations, as suggested by Barwise and Perry.[8] The argument shows that *any* pur-

6. Neale, "The Philosophical Significance of Gödel's Slingshot," pp. 761–825.

7. Gödel, "Russell's Mathematical Logic," p. 130.

8. Jon Barwise and John Perry, *Situations and Attitudes* (Cambridge, Mass.: MIT Press, 1983).

ported truth-makers we may think of will suffer the same fate, for what it shows is that whatever sentences are thought to correspond to, all true sentences must correspond to the same thing. Of course, it remains meaningful to say that true sentences or beliefs correspond to "the facts"; like the remark that true sentences are true because of "the way things are," this means no more than that they are true, with perhaps a hint that truth is an objective property. Some properties are aptly defined in terms of relations: the property of being a father is explained by the relation of father to offspring—the property holds if and only if the relation does. But the property of being true (or the one-place predicate 'is true') is not explained by the relation of correspondence. The reason is that if there is at most one thing to which sentences can correspond, we say no more when we say 'corresponds to the truth' than we say by the simpler 'is true'. We explain the application of a one-place predicate by reference to a relation only when there is an indefinitely large number of distinct entities to which the relation bears. There are no such entities available in the case of sentences, beliefs, judgments, or sentential utterances. It is important that truth, as applied to things in this world (utterances of sentences, inscriptions, beliefs, assertions), is a unitary property, for it is this that ties it so closely to the problem of predication. A large part of the problem of predication is, after all, just the problem of specifying what it is about predicates that explains why the sentential expressions in which they occur may be used to say something that is true or false.

Frege has been mentioned a number of times in these pages; it is time we turned to his views on predication. Frege was clear that if sentences are to function in language as they do—as the vehicles of assertion, command, question, and so on—they must be units of some sort. Therefore their components, roughly what we think of as words, must be shown to compose such units. Names frequently have the function of picking out or identifying objects which a sentence may go on to say something about. That this is the primary and exemplary role of names, there can be no doubt. This does not account for names which have no reference; Frege had relatively little to say about non-referring names, and he considered it a defect in natural languages that there should be such. (He counted definite descriptions as names, but treated definite descriptions in such a way that they always had exactly one referent.) There is clearly much more to be said about names. Nevertheless, it must be granted that their part in helping us to say things by uttering sentences is relatively clear, at least compared with the part played by predicates.

Frege's consuming interest in logic and the foundations of mathematics encouraged him to form a new and clearer view of the nature of predicates. Consider first operations like that of adding. This operation is expressed by the plus sign. But a plus sign by itself has no role until numerals are placed on each side of it; then the resulting expression stands for a number, eight, for example, if the numerals are '5' and '3'. This thought leads to the realization that we should think of the plus sign as containing two spaces, one to the left and one to the right, which are really *part* of the expression. We can write in '*x*' and '*y*' to keep track of these spaces, but these letters do not name anything: they simply mark the spaces.[9] Being clear about the spaces becomes important when we want to distinguish between, say, '*x* times *x*' and '*x* times *y*': the first expresses the operation of squaring, the second that of multiplication generally. The plus sign and the sign for multiplication are functional expressions, as is the sign for a negative number. The first two express the operations of mapping two numbers onto their sum and onto their product, and the third expresses the operation of mapping a number onto its negative. Frege called such functional expressions "incomplete" or "unsaturated." They are incomplete in the sense that

9. The letters at the end of the alphabet used to mark the spaces in a predicate should be considered part of the predicate; the use of the same letters as the variables of quantification is entirely different.

they carry blanks or empty spaces with them. They are completed by filling in the blanks; the result of filling in all the blanks is a singular term. Frege suggested the following analogy to aid in grasping his idea: Divide a line at some point. The point itself must go with one of the segments or the other. The lucky segment, which gets the point, is complete; the other segment is incomplete. This is, of course, a metaphor like the words 'incomplete' and 'unsaturated' themselves. Needless to say, there are non-mathematical functional expressions like 'the capital of x', 'the father of y', or 'the midpoint between x and y'. As remarked earlier, possessives ending in apostrophe 's' are functional expressions.

Frege noted that predicates are incomplete in much the way functional expressions are: they contain blanks to be filled in with names or quantified variables.[10] This leads to the simplified notion of a predicate which is current in modern logic: a predicate is any expression obtained from a sentence by subtracting one or more singular terms. Thus predicates are like functional expressions; one gets a functional expression by deleting one or more singular terms from expressions like '5+8'. Since '5+8' is a complete expression obtained by filling the blanks of a plus sign (a functional expression) with names of numbers, it seemed natural to Frege to propose taking predicates as functional expressions which become complete when the blank or blanks are filled in. This move ensures the unity of the sentence: each sentence refers, like any completed functional expression, to some one entity. But what entities should these be? Church believed that the Slingshot was implicit in Frege. The assumptions from which the Slingshot follows, including the assumption that definite descriptions are singular terms, are Fregean, and the conclusion that all true sentences, if they name anything, name the same thing, is Fregean. But the assumptions and conclusion of the Slingshot do not say *what* entity true sentences name or what

10. Frege uses the word 'predicate' for only one-place predicates; I follow contemporary practice.

entity false sentences name. Frege's thesis was that all true sentences name an entity he called *The True* and all false sentences name *The False*.

Here is the line of thought that led Frege to his view of the reference of a sentence. Singular terms with different senses can refer to the same object, and in complex singular terms, if we substitute a contained singular term for a co-referring term, the containing singular term will refer to the same object. If we know that a sentence contains a name, say 'Odysseus', and do not know or care whether the name has a reference, we do not inquire whether the sentence is true. "It is the striving for truth," Frege declares, "that drives us always to advance from the sense to the reference . . . We are therefore driven into accepting the truth-value of a sentence as constituting its reference."[11] We must agree that the truth value of a sentence is often what we care about, and if we accept the distinction between the meaning and the referent of a sentence we need not accept the conclusion that Russell feared, that all true sentences mean the same thing. We can also admire the elegant simplicity of Frege's late semantics: singular terms and functional expressions have senses and referents, and the senses of the parts of singular terms determine the senses of the complex terms in which they appear, just as the referents of the parts of terms determine the referents of the complex terms of which they are parts. Sentences emerge as singular terms, and truth-functional connectives for once earn their title to be called functional expressions, since they map truth values onto truth values.

Whether or not we think Frege's solution to the problem of predication is satisfactory, we should celebrate the attempt. Of all the efforts to account for the role of predicates that we have reviewed, Frege's is the only one that, by its treatment of predicates, clearly makes sentences semantic units. Of the attempts we have consid-

11. Gottlob Frege, "On Sense and Meaning," in *Translations from the Philosophical Writings of Gottlob Frege,* 3rd ed., ed. P. Geach and M. Black (Oxford: Basil Blackwell, 1980), pp. 56–78; p. 63.

ered, Frege alone has assigned a semantic role to predicates which promises to explain how sentences are connected to truth values. This impressive result could not have been achieved except in the context of modern logic, in the development of which Frege played a major role. It is not easy to imagine how any of these deep insights could have been arrived at in the absence of the others.

But does Frege's semantics solve the problem of predication? There remain serious problems. One was pointed out by Frege: the entities referred to by predicates cannot be objects, like the entities referred to by singular terms, for if they were, sentences would be strings of names, and the usual problem of how a sentence could constitute a unit would once more emerge. Frege therefore stressed the contrast between the referents of singular terms ('objects') and the referents of predicates ('concepts' in the case of one-place predicates, 'relations' in the case of two-place predicates). The distinction was reflected in grammar and (more clearly) in Frege's notation. Yet here, Frege admits, we face a dilemma, for as soon as we say anything about a concept we convert it into an object.[12] We say correctly that the city of Berlin is a city, but it is false that the concept *horse* is a concept, since any entity referred to by a definite description must be an object.[13] Part of the difficulty is that although objects cannot be predicative in nature, concepts and relations can be both predicative in nature and also fall under second-order concepts.[14] Frege attributed these embarrassments to an awkwardness of natural language, but he was clearly bothered:

12. A better way to put this, Frege remarks, is that when we talk about a concept or a relation we don't "convert" it into an object, but it comes to be "represented" by an object. Gottlob Frege, "On Concept and Object," in *Translations from the Philosophical Writings of Gottlob Frege,* 3rd ed., ed. Geach and Black, pp. 42–55; p. 46.

13. Ibid.

14. Frege admits that there is something misleading in using the same phrase 'fall under' in both cases, and suggests that perhaps we should say an object falls *under* a (first-order) concept, but a concept falls *within* a second-level concept. Frege, "On Concept and Object," pp. 50–51.

By a kind of necessity of language, my expressions, taken literally, sometimes miss my thought; I mention an object, when what I intend is a concept. I fully realize that in such cases I was relying upon a reader who would be ready to meet me halfway—who does not begrudge a pinch of salt.[15]

Michael Dummett says that soon after writing this Frege realized there was a way around the "awkwardness":[16] one should simply drop the pretense that the words 'concept', 'function', and 'relation' can form meaningful predicates with the addition of the copula; Frege had already adopted a notation in which the difficulty could not arise. Dummett adds that, although Frege did not do so, there is no difficulty in devising an expression in natural language that refers to whatever a predicate does. Thus in the sentence 'A philosopher is what 'x is a philosopher' stands for', the phrase 'what 'x is a philosopher' stands for' refers to the concept referred to by 'x is a philosopher' which is, for example, what Plato and Aristotle were. The grammar here is precisely what Strawson used to substantiate his claim, contra Quine, that we can quantify into predicate positions; the difference is that Dummett is clear that the predicate 'ε is what 'x is a philosopher' stands for' is a second-level predicate, which, as he points out, is exactly what Quine said. It follows that one cannot simply quantify into a first-order predicate position, for example, '(∃x)(Socrates x)': the grammar changes and so does the range of the variables.[17]

Dummett holds that these measures save Frege's ontology from the threat of incoherence; but another objection looms. Dummett

15. Ibid., p. 54.
16. Michael Dummett, *Frege: Philosophy of Language,* 2nd ed. (Cambridge, Mass.: Harvard University Press, 1981), pp. 212ff.
17. It is clear that the syntactic problem can be solved by legislation, but I do not see that Dummett's grammatical proposal works. 'What 'x is a philosopher' stands for' seems clearly to be understood as a singular term; it cannot be substituted for the predicate 'x is a philosopher' in 'Dummett is a philosopher' without turning it into a predicate with the addition of 'is'.

does not accept Frege's assimilation of sentences to complex singular terms (what Frege calls 'names'), calling this "a retrograde step" in Frege's thinking, a "ludicrous deviation," a "gratuitous blunder," and a "misbegotten doctrine."[18] Treating sentences as names, Dummett complains, obscures "the crucial fact that the utterance of a sentence, unlike that of a complex term, . . . can be used to effect a linguistic act, to make an assertion, give a command, etc."[19] I think this is clearly right: sentences do not have the kind of unity that names do. But if the idea that sentences are names is abandoned, neither sentential connectives nor predicates can stand for functions. If predicates do not refer to functions, then Frege's bold proposal is not a solution to the problem of predication.

Thus Dummett repudiates the idea that what predicates and the "truth-functional" connectives refer to are functions, but he retains the idea that these expressions have a "functional character." Real functions map objects onto objects (as before), but concepts and relations map objects onto truth values, and truth functions map truth values onto truth values. Dummett agrees with Frege that ordinary functional expressions, predicates, and sentential connectives have a semantical nature completely different from that of names or sentences in that they are incomplete. Sentences, more evidently than names, are complete; but since they are not names, Dummett introduces a third major semantical category, truth values, which are neither unsaturated nor objects. If Frege's syntax is modified to accommodate Dummett's semantic suggestions, expressions like '4 = snow is white' will not be sentences, as they were in Frege's syntax.[20]

18. Dummett, *Frege: Philosophy of Language*, pp. 7, 184, 196.
19. Ibid., p. 7.
20. Ibid., pp. 184–185. See also Dummett's *The Interpretation of Frege's Philosophy* (London: Duckworth, 1981), p. 249. It is not entirely clear to what extent Dummett is committed to the idea that functional expressions of these three sorts have referents. In *The Interpretation of Frege's Philosophy* he says,

Giving up the thesis that predicates are functional expressions and sentences are singular terms does not, Dummett insists, mean that we have to abandon the idea that predicates have referents. One thing that the referent of a predicate cannot be, however, is an abstract universal or relation, both because it cannot be an object and because, since it belongs to the "realm of reference," it cannot be abstract.[21] But what is it if not a function? Dummett settles for the idea that truth functions and concepts and relations are "analogous" to functions because, like functions, they are incomplete, and because they are "functional in nature" in the way they "map" entities onto entities.

In *The Interpretation of Frege's Philosophy* Dummett explains the deep insight he now finds in treating predicates and sentential connectives as functional in character, an aspect of Frege's late semantics which Dummett says he "seriously undervalued" in *Frege: Philosophy of Language*.[22] The idea is to generalize Frege's semantics in a way that accommodates an indefinite number of semantic

---

"There can be no objection to the functional conception of concepts; their predicative nature is fully catered for under this conception . . . What, in [*Frege: Philosophy of Language*], I failed to recognize is that, when due allowance is made for the distinction between objects and truth-values, the functional conception of concepts is, when rightly considered, inescapable, and provides *the* correct account of their incompleteness . . . If the referent of a sentence is taken to be a truth-value, then that of a predicate must be a mapping from objects to truth-values. Only such an account reflects faithfully what it is that constitutes the basic mode of employment of predicates in a language." This is not inconsistent with the remark that there "is no doubt that in general there *is* something which an incomplete expression stands for," from *Frege: Philosophy of Language*, p. 254. On the other hand, the modified version in *The Interpretation of Frege's Philosophy* can be read as not requiring that truth values be entities.

21. "What Frege was trying to avoid, by his doctrine of the incompleteness of concepts, relations, and functions, is the problem of 'how universals are related to particulars' . . . For Frege, the problems are entirely spurious . . . A concept and an object . . . need no glue to fit them together." Dummett, *Frege: Philosophy of Language,* pp. 174–175.

22. Dummett, *The Interpretation of Frege's Philosophy,* p. 166.

values that may be assigned to sentences, true and false (for Frege), two or more for other logics and semantic theories. Individual variables are assigned a chosen domain ("circumscribed or not") of objects, individual constants objects in the domain, and each function-letter a function from and into objects in the domain. Decisions are made as to the possible semantic values of sentences, and as to what are to be taken as the logical constants. At this point, "there remains no further choice about what the semantic value, under a given interpretation, of a predicate is taken to be. It can be nothing else but a function from the domain [of objects] to the set of possible semantic values of sentences."[23]

One cannot but be struck with the shift from emphasis on the referents of expressions to an emphasis on the "semantic values" of expressions. In *Frege: Philosophy of Language* Dummett had distinguished "reference as semantic role" and the identification of the referent of a name with its bearer. It was the failure of the analogy between the referential character of names and sentences that prompted his negative response to Frege's identification of predicates with functional expressions. Now he appreciates the extent to which the mapping character of sentential connectives and predicates can apply to semantic values as well as objects. Sentences have a semantic value, but semantic values are not objects.

This is an attractive move. Thinking of the referents of predicates as *any* sort of entity was bound to engender worries about how, in a simple sentence like 'Theaetetus sits', Theaetetus and the entity referred to by the predicate were related. It did not assuage these worries to be told that the question couldn't arise because of the unsaturated character of functions. No one can object to asking for a clear description of the "semantic values" of expressions so long as this means no more than asking about their semantic roles. As I understand it, taking this line marks a radical departure from Frege's

23. Ibid., pp. 167–168.

semantics. If we take predicates as referring to entities, we introduce a shadowy level of explanatory machinery between expressions and the work they do. The contrast with names is strange: with names we go straight to objects named. Or not quite straight, if we follow Dummett and Frege, for the senses or meanings of names mediate between expression and object. But if predicates have a referent, this is *in addition* to their sense and extension. This is the wheel that becomes redundant: to describe the semantic value of a predicate is not to introduce another level of explanation.[24]

As far as the Fregean explanation of predication is concerned, what is left, then, is the analogy between predicates and functional expressions. The predicate 'x sits' maps Theaetetus onto the truth value of 'Theaetetus sits'. Since truth values are not objects, we might say only that the predicate 'x sits' is such that, when appended to the name 'Theaetetus', it constitutes a sentence that is true or false (or perhaps has some other truth value). In other words, the predicate does just what we know predicates do. I do not question that predicates and functional expressions are in a way syntactically similar, or that the many metaphors ("mapping," "falling under," etc.) appeal to genuine intuitions. What I do question is whether predication has now been explained. Frege has greatly advanced our understanding of the problem by providing, for the first time, a syntax and logic that invite a precise semantics, by attempting an informal semantics that connects the semantic roles of expressions with the truth values of the sentences in which

24. What I describe as a departure from Frege is pretty much what Joan Weiner takes to be the correct interpretation of Frege. "Frege's notion of a term's having Bedeutung amounts to a demarcation of sharp boundaries for the application of the term and the indication of the epistemological roots of truths expressed by sentences in which the term appears." Weiner, *Frege in Perspective* (Ithaca: Cornell University Press, 1990), p. 190. "Ultimately, his reader's understanding of concept/object regimentation must come from their understanding of correct inference and how Frege's regimentation marks off constituents that play logical roles in inferences." Ibid., p. 250.

they occur, and by making clear the hopelessness of explaining the role of predicates by associating them with universals or other "objects." Frege was unique in his awareness of the problem of predication, but he did not solve it.[25]

25. [Davidson added the following note about this chapter: "My decision not to talk about Wittgenstein's view needs a comment. The reason is simply that try as I may I cannot satisfy myself that I have a sufficiently justified opinion what his views on predication were. I lament my failure here (as no doubt elsewhere) to fill in an important piece of the picture. There were clearly portentous exchanges between Frege and Wittgenstein, and between Wittgenstein and Russell. I have touched on some of the consequences of these exchanges, though of course I do not know exactly what they contained."]

CHAPTER 7

A Solution

The problem of predication has been at least vaguely grasped by many philosophers from the time of Plato to the present, and it was clearly understood and confronted by Frege. A plausible solution has also been known for some time. Yet though problem and solution have been rubbing elbows in society for some seventy years, they have never, so far as I know, been properly introduced. Or perhaps they have, and no one has told me. In any case, no harm will be done if I arrange a meeting.

Reviewing the history of the problem has revealed a number of important conditions that a satisfactory solution must meet. These I have rather arbitrarily organized under four heads.

First, a satisfactory account of predication depends on relating it to the truth of sentences. The reason is simple. If we cannot say how predicates contribute to the truth or falsity of the sentences in which they occur, there is little point in going on to the question of the unity of what a sentence expresses. Truth is the key to the unity of the acts we perform by uttering sentences, whether we are interested in giving information, giving a command, or asking a question. Of course there are many uses of sentences which are not intended to convey the truth; the point is rather that whatever our intention may be, what we say will not be understood by someone who does not know under what conditions it would be true. This holds even when neither the speaker nor the speaker's audience has an interest in whether what is said is true, as in story-telling, play-acting, or political campaigning. The relation between truth conditions and commands or questions is perhaps less direct than in the case of declarative sentences. Nevertheless, there is an obvious connection. It is essential to understanding an imperative to know what would be true if it were used to issue an order and the order was obeyed, and it is essential to understanding an interrogative to know what would constitute truthful or false answers, though of course we may not know which is which.

Of course there are those who question the importance of knowing the truth conditions of sentences in the understanding of those sentences. Such questioners are faced with the problem of saying in what the unity of a sentence consists. One reaction has been to turn from the extensional to the intensional and point, with Frege, to the meaning or sense of the terms in a sentence to explain the sense of the sentence as a whole—what Frege called the thought, and what some have called the proposition. This would be a convincing rejoinder if we had a distinct idea of what senses or meanings are. Until we do, it seems wise to deal with the twin issues of unity and predication at the extensional level, the level of semantics. The semantics of predicates is not solved by saying that there is a range of entities of which they are true, but this much does seem clearly right. Similarly, we are also clear, from the ostensive way in which the references of some names are learned, that some names have a reference. In these cases it is impossible not to concede that a simple sentence like 'Theaetetus sits' is true if and only if Theaetetus is (timelessly) in the extension of the predicate 'x sits'. This is so because in this case we know the person the name identifies, and we know what it is for someone to be seated. The sole point of meanings, whatever they are, is to allow us to identify the entity named, and to understand what it is for something to fall within the extension of the predicate. No doubt there are many cases where we understand predication that are not this simple, and the question of whether a sentence has a truth value is in doubt. But we arrive at this problem only because we understand the plainer cases where, on the basis of what we understand, we know the truth conditions of the utterance of a sentence. Whatever it is we know when we understand words, if this did not lead us in typical cases to grasp what it would be for an utterance to be true or false, there would be no point in understanding the words.

I have tried to phrase these remarks in a way that leaves open the question whether there are sentences, utterances of which we understand, for example sentences with names that do not name anything, which are neither true nor false. The point is that we would not understand the role of proper names in such sentences if we did not have the paradigmatic cases (as Dummett calls them) in which proper names do name someone or something. If we want to postulate entities such as meanings and propositions, we can explain what these entities are only insofar as we can explain how singular terms refer to objects and predicates are true of objects. There is no point in supposing we can *first* provide a clear account of meanings and on that basis arrive at an account of naming or reference, and of predication. The unity conferred on sentential utterances by the relations of words to objects is primary, and is based from the start on the model of utterances that are true or false. We cannot solve the problem of predication by speculating about the unity of the proposition if by 'proposition' we have in mind the sense or meaning of a sentence.

The *second* lesson which the history of attempts to provide a semantics for predicates teaches us is that associating predicates with objects such as universals, properties, relations, or sets will not solve the problem because it will always lead to an infinite regress. Plato and Aristotle sensed this when they insisted that every sentence had to include a verb, although this left them troubled about the relation between verbs and the forms or universals. If we insist that a universal is always involved in predication, then we need to interpret the copula, or perhaps just the space between singular term and predicative noun or adjective, as expressing a relation. But as Aristotle noted, if it is true that Socrates is wise, there seems to be only one object, wise Socrates, that makes it true. Suspicion of relations led Parmenides, Leibniz, Bradley, and others to embrace one or another form of monism; much of the motivation for such moves may be traced back to failure to solve the problem of predication. Hume rather lightheartedly confessed that having reduced the mind to a collection of isolated atoms, he saw no way to put them back together; one way of viewing this impasse is to realize that Hume had no way of accounting for the unity of thoughts with a sentential content. Russell, following Moore in promoting the possibility of logical analysis against the anti-analytic monism of Bradley, started by boldly breaking up what he called propositions into their component parts, objects (to correspond to true names), properties, and relations. Russell realized that this left the problem of uniting the parts. At first he waffled, saying that sometimes predicates just denote properties or relations, but that at least one predicate in a sentence must act *as* a verb. In the end he gave up this view without finding a better explanation for the role of predicates.

Frege was keenly aware of the problem, and he met it head on with his thesis that predicates are functional expressions and sentences are names of truth values. This gives the sentence a genuine unity, the unity of a complex singular term. Frege seemed uneasy with this solution, but I think for the wrong reason. Frege's reason was that he thought functional expressions should, if not name objects, at least refer to entities of some sort (for one thing, he wanted to be able to quantify over whatever predicates referred to). These entities could not be objects, for then predicates would be names, and the vicious regress would be reinstated. So there are entities that are not objects. The best Frege could do was to relapse into metaphor: the entities were "incomplete," "unsaturated." Frege remarks, "It must indeed be recognized that here we are confronted by an awkwardness of language, which I admit cannot be avoided, if we say that the concept *horse* is not a concept."[1] This is more than a superficial difficulty: if, as Frege maintained, predicates refer to entities, and this fact exhausts their semantic role, it does not matter how odd or permeable some of the entities are, for we can still raise the question of how these entities are related to those other entities, objects.

I say this was the wrong reason for Frege to be worried, because the claim that predicates refer to anything at all can be given up without direct cost to Frege's account of predication. (I do not say that other aspects of his philosophy would not have to be surrendered at the same time.) The right reason, at least from the present point of view, would have been that sentences do not play the same role in language as singular terms do, and if sentences are not singular terms, then predicates are not functional expressions.

The *third* lesson, which follows from the second, is that it is essential to separate the obvious observation that predicates introduce generality into sentences from the thought that predicates must at the same time introduce universals or other abstract entities into the subject matter of the sentence. Although Frege made this distinction absolutely clear by his notation, Frank Ramsey either was not aware of Frege, or was unconvinced, when he wrote his 1925 article "Universals."[2] There he argues that there is no deep distinction between particulars and universals, and that in this respect grammar misleads us. He observes that in the sentence 'Socrates is wise' 'Socrates' is the subject, but in 'Wisdom is a characteristic of Socrates' 'wisdom' is the subject, and he claims that these two

1. Gottlob Frege, "On Concept and Object," in *Translations from the Philosophical Writings of Gottlob Frege*, 3rd ed., ed. P. Geach and M. Black (Oxford: Basil Blackwell, 1980), pp. 42–55; p. 46.

2. Frank Plumpton Ramsey, "Universals," in *Philosophical Papers,* ed. D. H. Mellor (Cambridge: Cambridge University Press, 1990).

sentences express the same proposition.[3] Ramsey is right, of course, that universals are particulars as much as Socrates is, and that we can quantify into a position where a universal is named just as we can into a position occupied by the name 'Socrates'. His difficulty springs from assuming that a sentence like 'Socrates is wise' names both Socrates and the universal Wisdom. This leads to the familiar confusion about the copula and the "tie" that holds a "fact" together:

> 'q characterizes a' means no more or less than 'a is q,' it is merely a lengthened verbal form; and since the relation of characterization is admittedly not a constituent of 'a is q' it cannot be anything at all. As regards the tie, I cannot understand what sort of a thing it could be, and prefer Wittgenstein's view that in the atomic fact the objects are connected together without the help of any mediator. This does not mean that the fact is simply the collection of its constituents but that it consists in their union without any mediating tie.[4]

To recognize that it is necessary to distinguish between sentences that do and sentences that do not refer to abstract entities is not to say that properties, relations, and so forth do not exist. The existence of abstract objects is a separate issue. The point of the lesson is that their existence does not help to explain predication.[5]

3. Here we have an unusual reversal. It is usually thought that propositions, which are akin to meanings, divide more finely than extensional semantics, but Ramsey claims that these sentences express the same proposition where extensional semantics reveals a different subject matter.

4. Ramsey, "Universals," p. 29.

5. [Charles Parsons comments: "Davidson rightly distinguishes the question of the existence of properties and related abstract objects and the semantic role of predicates. For example, he doesn't seem ready to give up the idea that predicates have extensions but doesn't explain how that possibility fits into his scheme of things. The question is addressed in some of my writings: Essays 8 and 9 of *Mathematics in Philosophy: Selected Essays* (Ithaca: Cornell University Press, 1983) and "Objects and Logic," *The Monist* 65 (1982): 491–516. This question is one that a friend of the idea of predicates in some way designating objects would naturally raise."]

The *fourth* lesson is that the full scope and nature of the problem of predication emerges only in conjunction with a clear conception of the logical form of sentences. Until we have such a conception, we will be unsure what to count as a singular term or as a predicate. Confusion over the role of the copula is an example. Plato was right to emphasize two-word sentences like 'Theaetetus sits', but trouble immediately arises if we take 'sits' as referring to a Form, for as Plato saw we must then take the sentence as expressing the idea that Theaetetus *participates in* (or has some other relation to) the Form. When a copula is present, it may be taken to make explicit what is implicit when it is absent. In either case, though, the implicit or explicit element is what then needs explaining. The futility of endlessly introducing new entities to explain what holds a sentence together led Russell, after his frustration with the dual role of verbs, to treat sentences in effect as strings of names and to say it is the judging mind that joins the things named as related in a certain way. This entails that what unifies a sentence is no part or aspect of the sentence. There may be a deep truth in this rather Wittgensteinian thought, but it cannot be that the role of predicates is only to be explained by denying that they are, or contain, verbs.

The semantic role of the copula, or its lack of one, is only one conundrum that a correct theory of logical form resolves. It was Frege who rescued logic and semantics from the Aristotelian notion that phrases like 'a man', 'all men', and 'some men' are significant terms which can be treated indifferently as subjects or predicates, and who led us to recognize that not all predicates have only one position open for the insertion of a singular term. Putting these last points together helps to disclose the role of quantifiers and variables, and yields Frege's definition of a predicate: any expression got from a sentence by removing one or more singular terms.

Curiously, however, a systematic syntax adequate to the demands of modern logic and sensitive to a great deal of the expressive power of natural languages, coupled with a systematic semantics like Frege's, and even a semantics capable of defining logical truth and proving that rules of inference are valid, do not necessarily add up to a satisfactory explanation of predication.[6] What, then, does? The hardest part of the answer is provided by the technique for defining truth spelled out for the first time in Tarski's *Wahrheitsbegriff,* presented to the Warsaw Scientific Society on March 21, 1931, and published in Polish and German in 1933 and 1936 respectively. As far as I know, Tarski had little idea that he had in effect solved the problem of predication that had been puzzling philosophers for millennia; he certainly made no such claim.[7] Part of the explanation is no doubt Tarski's conviction that it was pointless to try to apply formal semantic methods to natural languages. His reason was the semantic paradoxes; he held that natural languages can apply a truth predicate of the language to any sentence in

6. This is so because the "standard semantics" adequate to define logical truth and prove the validity of rules of inference interprets predicates by assigning sets to them.

7. Solomon Feferman, in "Tarski's Conceptual Analysis of Semantical Notions" (paper delivered at the conference "Sémantique et épistémologie," Casablanca, April 24–26, 2002), maintains that there was no compelling logical reason for Tarski's work on the concept of truth and suggests that the motivation was a combination of psychological and programmatic factors. "Clearly," writes Feferman, "Tarski thought that as a side result of his work on definability and truth in a structure (which was of interest to mathematicians), he had something important to tell the philosophers that would straighten them out about the troublesome semantic paradoxes such as the Liar." Nowhere does Feferman credit Tarski with having solved the problem of predication, nor do the few philosophers (Karl Popper, Rudolph Carnap, Max Black, Michael Dummett) who criticized or admired Tarski's work on truth. Carnap mentions Tarski's method of defining truth for a language in *Introduction to Semantics,* but his sketch assigns properties to predicates, and makes no use of the concept of satisfaction. In Carnap's subsequent *Meaning and Necessity* the semantic "method of extension and intension" which dominates the work makes no basic use of Tarski's work, and cannot not be reconciled with it. [Parsons comments: "Davidson wants to treat semantic paradoxes like the set theoretical ones. What is needed for such a treatment is to make plausible an interpretation of natural language in terms of some hierarchy such as Tarski's language levels."]

that same language, and therefore to sentences containing that very predicate. This leads, under normal conditions, to a contradiction. Eliminating this threat involved departing from what Tarski called the "universality" of natural languages by making a distinction between the language for which he was defining truth and the language in which the definition was formulated.

No doubt it was partly because of Tarski's insistence that his truth definitions could not be applied to natural languages that philosophers, even those who understood it, showed little interest in his work. Max Black wrote a dismissive review which pointed out correctly (amid a flurry of conflations of use and mention) that the general concept of truth had not been defined.[8] The *Wahrheitsbegriff* had, of course, insisted on the fact that, given assumptions that Tarski found natural, the general predicate '*s* is true in *L*' for variable '*L*' cannot be defined. Michael Dummett criticized the work on the ground that it did not say anything about the *point* of the concept of truth.[9] Hilary Putnam wrote that "as a philosophical account of truth, Tarski's theory fails as badly as it is possible for an account to fail."[10] The philosophical reception of his work, such as it was, saddened Tarski. In 1944 he published "The Semantic Conception of Truth," in which he tried to persuade philosophers that his truth definitions were relevant to their perennial concern with the concept of truth. This attempt failed almost completely, perhaps in part because Tarski omitted from his sketch of the formal method of the *Wahrheitsbegriff* the step which was the key to the solution of the problem of predication. The *Wahrheitsbegriff*

8. Max Black, *Language and Philosophy* (Ithaca: Cornell University Press, 1949), p. 104.

9. Michael Dummett, *Truth and Other Enigmas* (London: Duckworth, 1978), preface, and Dummett, "Truth," in *Truth and Other Enigmas,* pp. 1–24.

10. Hilary Putnam, "A Comparison of Something with Something Else," *New Literary History* 17 (1985–1986): 61–79; p. 64. There is a fuller account of philosophers' objections to Tarski's work on truth in Chapters 1, 2, and 3.

should have interested philosophers of language for a more general reason, for it provided for the first time a semantical method against which partial theories of the logical form of sentences in natural language could be tested.

Tarski believed that his work on truth was philosophically important. In "The Semantic Conception of Truth" he made clear that his intent was to characterize as nearly as possible our ordinary semantical concepts, concepts that, as he puts it, express "connexions between expressions of a language and the objects . . . referred to by these expressions." Speaking specifically of truth, he explains that he does not want to assign a new meaning to an old word, but to "catch hold of the actual meaning of an old notion." He concludes, "I do not have any doubts that our formulation does conform to the intuitive content of that of Aristotle." He admitted that the intuitive notion was vague and, of course, that some of its applications led to paradox. "In spite of all this," Tarski says, "I happen to believe that the semantic conception does conform to a considerable extent with the common-sense usage."[11]

Many philosophers have either applauded Tarski's work on truth as showing that the concept of truth is trivial, or dismissed the work on the ground that it is irrelevant to the philosophical concept. Both views are mistaken, in my opinion. It is clearly a mistake to call Tarski a disquotationist. Everyone quotes ''Snow is white' is true if and only if snow is white' and points out that the two sides of the bi-conditional are not only equivalent, but would be logically equivalent in the context of a Tarski-style truth definition. So, the complaint (or applause) goes, why bother with the quotation marks and the truth predicate: instead of saying that the sentence 'Snow is white' is true, we can be satisfied by remarking that snow is white. But as Tarski pointed out, this works only if we have the very sen-

---

11. Alfred Tarski, "The Semantic Conception of Truth," *Philosophy and Phenomenological Research* 4 (1944): 341–376; p. 360.

tence at hand that we want to call true. We often want to say of a sentence not at hand that it is true or false: 'You gave the right (true) answer to this question last night, but I can't remember what you said.' When Quine said that Tarski had shown that truth was disquotational he was pointing out that for a particular language, a defined truth predicate which happens to be disquotational covers all and just the true sentences of that language. This may sound mildly deflationary, but only because it neglects to mention the fact that Tarski's method applies equally to cases where the defined truth predicate belongs to a language that does not include the language to which that predicate applies.[12]

Dummett and Putnam both say that Tarski has not defined the general concept of truth. This is, of course, obvious: Tarski insisted on it. What he did was to define truth predicates for specific languages, one at a time. The significant objection is that Tarski has not said, or even attempted to say, what it is that different truth definitions have in common (aside from the "uniform method" for constructing such definitions).[13] As Dummett put it, it is as though we were given the definition of what it is to win in various games, but were given no hint as to what winning was, for example, that it is what one tries to do in playing. I agree with the point, but I do not see it as an objection to Tarski's work. It is not an objection because Tarski is counting on the fact, as he clearly says, that we already have a good, though partial, grasp of the concept of truth. This is why he counts on what he calls Convention-T to persuade us that what he has defined for his sample languages is the very con-

12. [Parsons comments (in his notes on the original manuscript): "Davidson conditionalizes the whole truth definition with: ('p' is true or 'p' is false) → ('p' is true if and only if p)." Davidson remarks: "Wonderful! This also takes care of names that don't name."]

13. Alfred Tarski, "The Concept of Truth in Formalized Languages," in *Logic, Semantics, Metamathematics,* ed. J. H. Woodger (New York: Oxford University Press, 1956), pp. 152–278; p. 153.

cept we have in mind. It is Convention-T that says a formally correct definition of a truth predicate for a language *L* must entail, for sentence *s* of *L,* a theorem of the form '*s* is true if and only if *p*', where for '*s*' we substitute a description of a sentence of *L,* and for '*p*' we substitute a sentence in the metalanguage which translates *s.* Tarski assumes that we will agree, on the basis of our prior understanding of the concept of truth, that such a predicate will apply to all and only the true sentences of *L;* otherwise he would have had no reason to claim that his definitions conform to common-sense usage. He realizes that we bring to his work on truth a grasp of the general, unrelativized concept which he has not tried to formulate. So there is more to say about the concept of truth than Tarski has said. This does not mean that what he has done is trivial, that it is philosophically uninteresting, or that it is unrelated to our understanding of the concept of truth.[14]

In an attempt to show that Tarski failed in his attempt to illuminate the concept of truth, it has been widely remarked that since the truth definitions make use of no semantic concepts, the resulting T-sentences, which have the form required by Convention-T, are logical truths, and so cannot tell us anything about the semantic properties of any real language. This is technically correct, of course, but it misses the point. Definitions are designed to indicate

14. [Parsons comments: "I would complain that Davidson gives too much philosophical credit to Tarski and too little to Quine and possibly himself. . . . The principal point relevant to the present issue that Davidson extracts from Tarski is that his method of characterizing truth works without assigning entities (properties, relations, or whatever} to predicates (or, for that matter, sentences). Even though Tarski was very sympathetic to the nominalism of Kotarbinski, he does not make the connection between this feature of his construction and issues about universals. The one who does is Quine, as Davidson seems to acknowledge in Chapter 5, although he gives Quine only a small role in the overall story. He can legitimately reproach Quine for not putting more stress on the contributions of Tarski and treating it simply as technical background, or as informative about truth more than predication. But the fact remains that Quine stated the central philosophical point clearly and applied it, as Tarski did not."]

how the defined expression can be eliminated from the contexts in which it appears. But when Tarski said he did not intend his definitions to foist a new meaning on an old word but to capture the common-sense meaning of an old notion, he meant that there is nothing in the formal apparatus to prevent us from asking ourselves whether one of his truth predicates picks out the true sentences in a language we understand. (The languages for which Tarski gave truth definitions were all interpreted languages.) When we ask ourselves this question, we are using our own concept of truth, which is general, and therefore not defined. It is not a question the definition aims to answer. We know, it should go without saying, that the informal concept we bring to this question may, given further natural assumptions, lead to contradictions. Nevertheless, trusting to our grasp of the concept, we can ask whether a particular truth definition does, in this sense, have an application.

When we inquire whether a truth definition defines the class of true sentences in a particular language, we are thinking of the truth definition as stipulating a possible language. If some actual language had the stipulated semantics, that is, if it were related to the world in the way a language so defined would be related to the world, how could we tell whether a speaker, or group of speakers, were speaking this language? The definition cannot answer this question, for it is an empirical question. But we understand the question if we understand, as it must be assumed we do, the language in which the definition is formulated and, of course, the general concept of truth. The relative clarity of this inquiry does not depend on the fact that Convention-T appeals to the obscure notion of translation; all we want to know is whether someone is speaking the language which a particular truth definition describes. This is tested (inductively, of course) by determining whether an adequate sample of T-sentences are deemed to be true when we take the truth predicate as meaning what our everyday predicate 'is true' means when applied to the sentences of the language.

A simpler way of putting the matter is to alter a Tarski-type truth

definition by removing the step which turns the recursive characterization of truth into an explicit definition, leaving an axiomatic theory in which the truth predicate is not defined, but is understood as
expressing our pretheoretical concept of truth. The theory then
states the truth conditions of the sentences of a language. It is clear
that it is an empirical question whether this theory applies to a particular language we understand. It is also clear that the theory implies no contradictions as long as the object language does not contain the same truth predicate. Such an axiomatic treatment of truth
would not have satisfied Tarski's Convention-T, which required a
"formally correct" definition of a predicate, employing no semantic
terms. The axiomatic version does, of course, contain a semantic
term, which is the truth predicate itself.

Further adjustments to such a theory must be made if it is to specify the truth conditions for the sentences of a natural language.
Many of the sentences of a natural language do not have fixed
truth conditions since different utterances of any sentence containing tensed verbs, demonstratives, or other indexical words may differ in truth from utterance to utterance. One way this difficulty can
be met is by relativizing the truth conditions of such sentences to a
time, place, speaker, and perhaps other parameters. Many further
problems arise when we try to accommodate the structures of natural languages to the devices available within an appropriate theory.
Since the question whether, or to what extent, such accommodation
is possible has been much discussed, I shall not pursue it here. If the
problem of predication can be solved for only as much of natural
language as we now know how to put into standard quantificational form (embellished with many of the most obvious deictic elements), an impressive start will have been made. It is unlikely that a
method that correctly describes the semantic role of predicates in
first-order predicate languages is irrelevant to languages with richer
resources.

How does Tarski's methodology solve the problem? The first

thing I claimed that we could learn from the history of failures was how central the concept of truth is to any solution. This is an insight many have had, but Frege could be said to be the first to appreciate the importance of the connection between truth and predication in the context of modern logic and a consistent, clearly specified semantics. The importance of the connection is this: if we can show that our account of the role of predicates is part of an explanation of the fact that sentences containing a given predicate are true or false, then we have incorporated our account of predicates into an explanation of the most obvious sense in which sentences are unified, and so we can understand how, by using a sentence, we can make assertions and perform other speech acts. Truth is the prime semantic concept; we could not think or speak in the sense of entertaining or communicating propositional contents without it. The semantics of names, functional expressions, complex singular terms, predicates, quantifiers, variables, and sentential connectives are all subsidiary to the work they do in explaining the truth conditions of sentences. Tarski's methods allow us to specify the roles of the smallest meaningful parts in an infinity of sentences in a way that allows us to prove, in the case of any sentence, what its truth conditions are. This is so because the number of smallest meaningful parts in the language is finite, and the number of roles is therefore finite. It is, of course, the role of predicates in this setup that interests us.

It should come as no surprise that Tarski provides no entities at all to which sentences correspond or which sentences name, picture, or otherwise represent. No facts appear in the official apparatus, nor do propositions, either as the meanings of sentences or as half-extensional, half-intensional entities in the world as in Russell's early theory. It is true that Tarski suggests, in his informal defense of the claim that his constructions capture the intuitive concept of truth, that his truth definitions embody the idea that true sentences correspond to the facts. But this is misleading, since in his work on truth there is nothing for sentences to correspond to. What he presumably has in mind is that his method does establish relations between significant parts of sentences and entities in the world, and shows how these relations are adequate to account for the truth conditions of sentences.

The second lesson that has been borne in on us again and again by our survey is that any attempt to give a full explication of the semantics of predicates by associating them with single objects of any kind is doomed. It does not matter what the objects are. Platonic ideas or Forms, Aristotelian universals, properties, characteristics, relations (in the case of two- or more-place predicates)—none of these provides a satisfactory account of the role of predicates.

It is important to be clear that if we try to explain the role of predicates by introducing entities to which they refer, it does not matter what we *call* the entities or how we describe them. We may distinguish as clearly and profoundly as we please between particulars and universals, between the job that singular terms do in identifying or individuating objects and the job that predicates do in introducing generality; we will still have to describe the semantic role of predicates. Nor will it help to distinguish, as Frege did, between objects, which is what singular terms refer to, and concepts, which is what one-place predicates refer to. To say that predicates are functional expressions, and are therefore incomplete or unsaturated, and that what they refer to is similarly full of holes or spaces waiting to be filled in, does not help: entities are entities, whatever we call them. Frege's syntax and metaphors emphasize that there is a fundamental difference between singular terms and predicates, but this difference cannot usefully be thought to consist in a difference in the entities to which they refer.

A theory of truth of the Tarskian sort I have described, like Tarski's truth definitions, does not explain the function of predicates by relating them to particular entities which somehow embody generality. This point has often been overlooked because the

standard semantics employed in proving that syntactically formulated rules of inference are valid, or that sentences syntactically
specified are logical truths, associates sets with predicates.[15] There
is nothing incorrect about such a method, but it is wrong to suppose the usefulness of this method shows that we can explain predication simply by associating predicates with sets. In effect, the
standard semantics employed understands such predications as
'Theaetetus sits' as 'Theaetetus is a member of the set of seated ob-

15. The alternative strategy available to Frege which Dummett seems to have
in mind is suggested by his mentioning several times what he calls the "standard" accounts of truth, or "the familiar semantics for quantificational language." Michael Dummett, *Frege: Philosophy of Language,* 2nd ed. (Cambridge, Mass.: Harvard University Press, 1981), p. 171. In such semantics,
"reference is that which has to be ascribed to the primitive expressions . . . individual constants, predicates, relational and functional expressions—in order to
give the truth-definition for the sentences of the language." Frege made such semantics standard, he says, and Tarski later made it far more explicit, and ex-
posed its set-theoretical foundations. The difference, which is enormous, is that
while Frege was interested in semantics for its own sake, modern logicians are
interested in the relation of logical consequence.

All this is, of course, correct, but it misses the point as far as the role of predicates is concerned. What Dummett calls "the familiar semantics" now recognized as needed in order to give a definition of truth for a language is actually
the semantics that serves to define truth in an interpretation, which is exactly
what is requisite for the study of logical consequence, and such a semantics
does indeed treat predicates in terms of the sets of objects which are their extensions under various interpretations. As Dummett says, "In the standard semantics, the interpretation of a predicate is a set" (ibid., p. 173). It is natural to
think that the interpretation which assigns to predicates the extensions they
have in the real world then defines truth for a real language. This was not, as
Dummett emphasizes, Frege's view: for him predicates refer to incomplete entities "in the real world; they are the extra-linguistic correlates of linguistic expressions; they are what we talk about" (ibid., p. 170). What I wish to stress is
that assigning sets to predicates cannot solve the problem of predication. Frege
was right not to accept what Dummett calls the standard semantics, for it does
not explain the role of predicates, and therefore cannot yield an adequate account of the unity of the sentence or of truth.

jects'. Since the method is extensional, we may let the identity of the sets determined by predicates make all the distinctions needed to articulate the concept of being true in an interpretation, and it is easy to specify all the interpretations in which a sentence is true by quantifying over sets. It is obvious, however, that the role of the original predicates has not been explained by this process. In the sentence 'Theaetetus is a member of the set of seated objects' the predicate 'sits' does not appear; the new predicate is the predicate 'is a member of', the semantic role of which is not given. We are back with Plato's problem of explaining the predicate 'instantiates' if we take a predicate like 'sits' to refer to or stand for a Form. The two-place predicates 'instantiates' and 'is a member of' are the expressions the roles of which we want to explain.

There can be no doubt that Tarski's truth definitions, and theories of truth based on them, clearly distinguish between the issue whether properties and other abstract entities exist and the semantic role of predicates. Of course, if some (second-level) predicates are true of abstract objects, those objects must exist, but their existence does not explain the role of such predicates. This replies to the third lesson we learned from the saga of failed attempts to explain predication. It is worth mentioning that, far from avoiding abstract entities, Tarski's method for characterizing truth makes use of set theory, and it is not easy to see how this can be avoided. But this unavoidable assumption of set theory and the existence of sets does not mean that predicates refer to or stand for sets. We must not confuse the ontology of the explanatory machinery with the ontology of expressions whose semantics we are describing, even if most of the vocabulary of the machinery belongs to the language the semantics of which we are describing.

The fourth lesson was that no account of predication could be considered a success which did not deal from the start with quantifiers and quantificational structure. Tarski's solution to the problem of predication certainly passes this test. It would not be an exaggeration to say that attending to the role of variables is the secret of Tarski's way of coping with predication. This is literally the case with the languages for which he defines a truth predicate, for they contain no individual constants. But when we extend the method to include languages with individual constants, then we must modify the description of the method to say the following: the secret is attending to the gaps or spaces in predicates, the gaps which come to be occupied by individual constants or the variables of quantification before predicates can make their contribution to the truth values of sentences.

So far, Tarski's method has not been distinguished from Frege's except that it associates no entities which express generality with predicates or any entities at all with sentences. The focus on the role of variables or the spaces they occupy is analogous to Frege's, and was inspired by him. Tarski's essential innovation is to make ingenious use of the idea that predicates are *true of* the entities which are named by the constants that occupy their spaces or are quantified over by the variables which appear in the same spaces and are bound by quantifiers. Because there is no particular limit to the number of free variables in a well-formed open sentence, Tarski introduces infinite sequences of the entities over which the variables range. Since both the sequences and the variables are ordered, any given sequence can be thought of as assigning entities to particular variables, as if those variables were performing the role of names. It is then possible to characterize the circumstances under which a given sequence assigns entities to the variables in a sentence which, were those variables the names of those entities, would create a true sentence. Such sequences are said to *satisfy* the sentence, whether the sentence be open or closed. For this characterization to apply to names, it is only necessary to count names in the same category as variables (let us call the items in this category 'singular terms'), and stipulate that all sequences assign the named entities to the appropriate names.

Spelling out the characterization of the satisfaction relation, which I shall not do here, requires several steps, each of which specifies the conditions under which a given sequence satisfies a sentence, open or closed. The steps involve axioms of two sorts. First, there is an axiom for each sentence with an unstructured predicate (its spaces filled with variables or names) specifying the conditions under which that sentence is satisfied by a particular sequence. There will be a finite number of such axioms, since the basic vocabulary of any language must be finite. Second, there will be axioms recursively characterizing the satisfaction conditions of sentences built up from simpler sentences by the operations of negation, alternation, and the other sentential connectives, and, of course, the quantifiers. Since closed sentences contain no free variables, true sentences will be satisfied by all sequences, and false sentences by none.

Tarski was able to turn this axiomatic characterization of satisfaction into an explicit definition of the satisfaction-predicate by employing some fancy set-theoretical apparatus, and this in turn leads to the explicit definition of the truth predicate. The set-theoretical power needed for the explicit definition required by Tarski cannot, of course, be available in the language for which truth is being defined, on pain of contradiction. I have forsworn the step which yields explicit definitions, and am therefore regarding Tarski's constructions as axiomatizations of the intuitive, and general, concept of truth. The result does not have the proven innocence of the defined concept, and thus would not, as I said, have been welcome to Tarski. This is the cost of being in a position to apply the method to actual languages.

It will be noted that I explained satisfaction in terms of truth. If I were out to define truth, this would be circular. But defining truth is not my aim, for it cannot be done. I was not defining but *using* the concept of truth, which, however beset by paradox, is the clearest and most basic semantic concept we have. What my strategy amounts to, then, is to show how our grasp of the concept of truth can explain predication. There is another semantic concept which went into the full account of the role of predicates, and that is the name-relation. It slipped in at the point where, in specifying the sequences needed to characterize satisfaction, each sequence paired names with the objects named.

Is the name-relation the sole point at which the entire construction is tied to the real world? No, for we quantify over endless unnamed entities. It is the name-relation which may be superfluous, either by use of Russell's theory of descriptions or in some other way. Any desired distinction between objects can be made if there is a one-place predicate, no matter how complex, which is true of one of the objects but not of the other. This was, of course, Russell's thought when he suggested that most of what are considered proper names should be supplanted by definite descriptions. I will return to this issue in a moment.

Has Tarski's method for defining truth predicates, modified in the way I have suggested, solved the problem of predication? It may be objected that it gives an account of how each predicate in a language contributes to the truth conditions of the sentences in which it occurs, but that it gives no general explanation of predication. It is true that no such general explanation emerges. What does emerge is a *method* for specifying the role of each and every predicate in a specific language; this role is given by a non-recursive axiom which says under what conditions it is true of any number of entities taken in the order in which its blanks occur. What more can we demand? I think the history of the subject has demonstrated that more would be less.

The story is not complete without an examination of how it is possible to tell whether a speaker, or group of speakers, is using a language defined by the method I have described. Since this is a matter I have examined at length elsewhere, I will say only a few words about it here. In the method described, truth is clearly the basic concept which must be given empirical application. This does not mean, of course, a way of telling when a sentence is true, but when a sentence is being treated by speakers as true or false. I do not think there is, or could be, a conventional mode of speaking which can be counted on to manifest this attitude. Frege was wrong to think that we could invent a sign to indicate that a sentence was being used to make an assertion, much less that it was being used to make a sincere assertion (every liar and actor would use it). Nevertheless, we frequently can tell when someone is making an honest assertion, or, more generally, when a speaker is uttering a sentence that he or she holds to be true. If this were not the case, we would never come to understand a language.

Rudimentary patterns of sentences held to be true can be employed to identify the logical constants, conjunction, negation, and the apparatus of quantification. Some names are learned by direct ostension and as if they were contained in sentences: what may be said aloud is just a name, understood as a short sentence ('This is Peter', 'That is Paul'). Names learned in this way are guaranteed a reference. Names learned less directly can then be treated as definite descriptions. This leaves predicates. As with names, some unstructured predicates must be learned by ostension: again what is uttered may be single words, treated as sentences ('This is green', 'That is a book'). Predicates less directly tied to perception are interpreted as they occur in sentences which also contain ostensibly learned predicates, or through their relations to sentences containing such predicates.

In these remarks, ostension is intended to be taken broadly. It covers the obvious cases where there is intentional teaching or a co-operative informant, but also cases where a community of speakers can simply be seen interacting in a mutually observed environment. The onlooking learner or interpreter picks things up.

The clues used by a learner of a first language and the data consciously sought by the field linguist are just what is needed to confirm, inductively, that a language in use is correctly described by a theory of truth based on Tarski's methodology. The concept of truth plays the leading role throughout. Ostensive learning, broadly conceived, depends either on the attempt on the part of teacher or informant to say what is true, or on the ability of the learner to detect when a speaker is saying what he or she holds to be literally true. Naturally, what is held to be true is not necessarily true. But the learner must assume in the case of ostension that what is held to be true *is* true until enough of the relations among sentences are in place to justify treating some ostensions as false. Thus the contribution of predicates to the truth conditions of sentences depends on and is explained by our grasp of the concept of truth.

Bibliography

Aristotle. *Categories and De Interpretatione,* trans. J. L. Ackrill. Oxford: Oxford University Press, 1963.

Barwise, Jon, and Perry, John. *Situations and Attitudes.* Cambridge, Mass.: MIT Press, 1983.

Black, Max. *Language and Philosophy.* Ithaca: Cornell University Press, 1949.

Bradley, Francis Herbert. *Appearance and Reality.* Oxford: Oxford University Press, 1897.

Brandom, Robert, ed. *Rorty and His Critics.* Oxford: Blackwell, 2000.

Burge, Tyler. "Frege on Truth." In *Frege Synthesized,* ed. L. Haaparanta and J. Hintikka, pp. 97–154. Dordrecht: Reidel, 1986.

—— "Individualism and the Mental." *Midwest Studies in Philosophy* 4 (1979): 73–121.

—— "Individualism and Psychology." *The Philosophical Review* 95 (1986): 3–45.

—— "Wherein Is Language Social?" In *Reflections on Chomsky,* ed. Alexander George, pp. 176–191. London: Basil Blackwell, 1989.

Cherniss, Harold. *Aristotle's Criticism of Plato and the Academy.* Baltimore: Johns Hopkins University Press, 1944.

Church, Alonzo. "Carnap's *Introduction to Semantics.*" *Philosophical Review* 52 (1943): 298–305.

—— *Introduction to Mathematical Logic,* vol. 1. Princeton: Princeton University Press, 1956.

Cornford, Francis MacDonald. *Plato's Theory of Knowledge.* London: Routledge, 1960.

Davidson, Donald. "Afterthoughts." *Subjective, Intersubjective, Objective,* pp. 154–158. New York: Oxford University Press, 2001.

———— "Belief and the Basis of Meaning." *Inquiries into Truth and Interpretation,* 2nd ed., pp. 141–154. New York: Oxford University Press, 2001.

———— "A Coherence Theory of Truth and Knowledge." *Subjective, Intersubjective, Objective,* pp. 137–153. New York: Oxford University Press, 2001.

———— "Comments on Karlovy Vary Papers." In *Interpreting Davidson,* ed. P. Kotatko, P. Pagin, and G. Segal, pp. 285–307. Stanford: CSLI, 2001.

———— "Communication and Convention." *Inquiries into Truth and Interpretation,* 2nd ed., pp. 265–280. New York: Oxford University Press, 2001.

———— "Empirical Content." *Subjective, Intersubjective, Objective,* pp. 159–176. New York: Oxford University Press, 2001.

———— "The Folly of Trying to Define Truth." *Journal of Philosophy* 93 (1996): 263–278.

———— *Inquiries into Truth and Interpretation,* 2nd ed. New York: Oxford University Press, 2001.

———— "Knowing One's Own Mind." *Subjective, Intersubjective, Objective,* pp. 15–38. New York: Oxford University Press, 2001.

———— "Meaning, Truth, and Evidence." In *Perspectives on Quine,* ed. R. Gibson. New York: Blackwell, 1989.

———— "Radical Interpretation." *Inquiries into Truth and Interpretation,* 2nd ed., pp. 125–140. New York: Oxford University Press, 2001.

———— *Rationality, Irrationality, and Value.* New York: Oxford University Press, forthcoming.

———— "The Structure and Content of Truth." *Journal of Philosophy* 87 (1990): 279–328.

———— "Thought and Talk." *Inquiries into Truth and Interpretation,* 2nd ed., pp. 155–170. New York: Oxford University Press, 2001.

———— "Three Varieties of Knowledge." *Subjective, Intersubjective, Objective,* pp. 205–220. New York: Oxford University Press, 2001.

———— "Toward a Unified Theory of Thought and Action." *Grazer Philosophische Studien* 11 (1980): 1–12. Reprinted in Davidson, *Rationality, Irrationality, and Value.* New York: Oxford University Press, forthcoming.

——— "True to the Facts." *Inquiries into Truth and Interpretation,* 2nd ed., pp. 37–54. New York: Oxford University Press, 2001.

——— "Truth and Meaning." *Inquiries into Truth and Interpretation,* 2nd ed., pp. 17–36. New York: Oxford University Press, 2001.

——— "What Is Quine's View of Truth?" *Inquiry* 37 (1994): 437–440.

——— "What Metaphors Mean." *Inquiries into Truth and Interpretation,* 2nd ed., pp. 245–264. New York: Oxford University Press, 2001.

Dewey, John. *Essays in Experimental Logic.* New York: Dover, 1953.

——— *Experience and Nature.* New York: Dover, 1958.

——— *Logic: The Theory of Inquiry.* New York: Holt, 1938.

——— *Reconstruction in Philosophy.* New York: Holt, 1920.

Diamond, Cora. *The Realistic Spirit.* Cambridge, Mass.: MIT Press, 1991.

——— "Truth before Tarski: After Sluga, after Ricketts, after Geach, after Goldfarb, Hylton, Floyd, and van Heijenoort." In *From Frege to Wittgenstein: Perspectives on Early Analytic Philosophy,* ed. Erich Reck, pp. 252–279. New York: Oxford University Press, 2002.

Dummett, Michael. *Frege: Philosophy of Language,* 2nd ed. Cambridge, Mass.: Harvard University Press, 1981.

——— *Frege: Philosophy of Mathematics*, 2nd ed. London: Duckworth, 1981.

——— *Frege and Other Philosophers.* Oxford: Oxford University Press, 1991.

——— *The Interpretation of Frege's Philosophy.* London: Duckworth, 1981.

——— "Truth." *Truth and Other Enigmas,* pp. 1–24. London: Duckworth, 1978.

——— *Truth and Other Enigmas.* London: Duckworth, 1978.

Etchemendy, John. "Tarski on Truth and Logical Consequence." *Journal of Symbolic Logic* 53 (1988): 51–79.

Feferman, Solomon. "Tarski's Conceptual Analysis of Semantical Notions." Paper delivered at the conference "Sémantique et épistémologie," Casablanca, April 24–26, 2002.

Field, Hartry. "The Deflationary Conception of Truth." In *Fact, Science, and Morality,* ed. C. Wright and G. MacDonald, pp. 55–117. New York: Blackwell, 1987.

——— "Deflationist Views on Meaning and Content." *Mind* 103 (1994): 249–285.

———— "Tarski's Theory of Truth." *Journal of Philosophy* 69 (1972): 347–375.

Fine, Arthur. "The Natural Ontological Attitude." In *The Shaky Game: Einstein, Realism, and the Quantum Theory,* 2nd ed., pp. 112–135. Chicago: University of Chicago Press, 1986.

Frede, Michael. "Aristotle on Nouns and Verbs in *De Interpretatione* 2–3." In *Aristotle's De Interpretatione,* ed. M. Frede and M. Mignucci. Oxford: Oxford University Press, forthcoming.

———— "Plato's Sophist on False Statements." In *The Cambridge Companion to Plato*, ed. R. Kraut, pp. 397–424. Cambridge: Cambridge University Press, 1992.

Frege, Gottlob. "Function and Concept." In *Collected Papers on Mathematics, Logic, and Philosophy*, ed. B. McGuiness, pp. 137–156. Oxford: Blackwell, 1984.

———— "On Concept and Object." In *Translations from the Philosophical Writings of Gottlob Frege,* 3rd ed., ed. P. Geach and M. Black, pp. 42–55. Oxford: Basil Blackwell, 1980.

———— "On Sense and Meaning." In *Translations from the Philosophical Writings of Gottlob Frege,* 3rd ed., ed. P. Geach and M. Black, pp. 56–78. Oxford: Basil Blackwell, 1980.

Geach, Peter. *Reference and Generality.* Ithaca: Cornell University Press, 1962.

———— "Truth and God." *Proceedings of the Aristotelian Society,* Supplementary Volume 61 (1982): 83–97.

Gödel, Kurt. "Russell's Mathematical Logic." In *The Philosophy of Bertrand Russell,* ed. P. A. Schilpp, pp. 123–153. Evanston, Ill.: Northwestern University Press, 1944.

Grice, H. Paul. "Meaning." *The Philosophical Review* 66 (1957): 377–388.

Hempel, Carl. "On the Logical Positivist's Theory of Truth." *Analysis* 2 (1935): 49–59.

Horwich, Paul. "Deflating Compositionality." In *Interpreting Davidson*, ed. P. Kotatko, P. Pagin, and G. Segal, pp. 95–109. Stanford: CSLI, 2001.

———— *Meaning.* Oxford: Oxford University Press, 1998.

———— "Three Forms of Realism." *Synthese* 51 (1982): 181–201.

———— *Truth.* Oxford: Blackwell, 1990.

Hume, David. *A Treatise of Human Nature,* ed. L. A. Selby-Bigge. Oxford: Oxford University Press, 1951.

Hylton, Peter. "The Nature of the Proposition and the Revolt against Idealism." In *Philosophy in History,* ed. R. Rorty, J. Schneewind, and Q. Skinner, pp. 375–397. Cambridge: Cambridge University Press, 1984.

James, William. *Pragmatism.* New York: Longmans & Green, 1907.

Jeffrey, Richard. *The Logic of Decision,* 2nd ed. Chicago: University of Chicago Press, 1983.

Kant, Immanuel. *Critique of Pure Reason,* trans. Norman Kemp Smith. New York: St. Martin's Press, 1965.

Kripke, Saul. *Wittgenstein on Rules and Private Language.* Cambridge, Mass.: Harvard University Press, 1982.

Leeds, Stephen. "Theories of Reference and Truth." *Erkenntnis* 13 (1978): 111–130.

Leibniz: Philosophical Writings, ed. G. H. R. Parkinson, trans. Mary Morris and G. H. R. Parkinson. London: J. M. Dent, 1973.

Lewis, C. I. *An Analysis of Knowledge and Valuation.* La Salle, Ill.: Open Court, 1946.

Linsky, Leonard. "The Unity of the Proposition." *Journal of the History of Philosophy* 30 (1992): 243–273.

McGuinness, Brian. *Wittgenstein: A Life: Young Ludwig, 1889–1921.* Berkeley: University of California Press, 1988.

Meinwald, Constance. *Plato's Parmenides.* Oxford: Oxford University Press, 1991.

Neale, Stephen. *Facing Facts.* Oxford: Oxford University Press, 2001.

——— "The Philosophical Significance of Gödel's Slingshot." *Mind* 104 (1995): 761–825.

Neurath, Otto. "Protokollsätze." *Erkenntnis* 3 (1932/33): 204–214.

Parsons, Charles. *Mathematics in Philosophy: Selected Essays.* Ithaca: Cornell University Press, 1983.

——— "Objects and Logic." *The Monist* 65 (1982): 491–516.

Patterson, Richard. *Aristotle's Modal Logic.* Cambridge: Cambridge University Press, 1995.

Plato. *Parmenides,* trans. W. R. M. Lamb and Robert Gregg Bury. London: Heinemann, 1926.

——— *Sophist,* trans. W. R. M. Lamb and Robert Gregg Bury. London: Heinemann, 1928.

Putnam, Hilary. "A Comparison of Something with Something Else." *New Literary History* 17 (1985–86): 61–79. Reprinted in *Words and Life,* ed. James Conant. Cambridge, Mass.: Harvard University Press, 1994.

—— "On Truth." In *How Many Questions?* ed. Leigh Cauman et al., pp. 35–56. Indianapolis: Hackett, 1983.

—— *Realism and Reason: Philosophical Papers,* vol. 3. New York: Cambridge University Press, 1983.

—— "Reference and Understanding." In *Meaning and Use,* ed. A. Margalit. Dordrecht: Reidel, 1979.

—— "Reply to Dummett's Comment." In *Meaning and Use,* ed. A. Margalit. Dordrecht: Reidel, 1979.

Quine, W. V. "On Empirically Equivalent Systems of the World." *Erkenntnis* 9 (1975): 313–328.

—— *Ontological Relativity and Other Essays.* New York: Columbia University Press, 1969.

—— *Philosophy of Logic,* 2nd ed. Englewood Cliffs, N.J.: Prentice-Hall, 1986.

—— "Progress on Two Fronts." *Journal of Philosophy* 93 (1996): 159–163.

—— "Reply to Roger F. Gibson Jr." In *The Philosophy of W. V. Quine,* ed. L. E. Hahn and P. A. Schilpp. Lasalle, Ill.: Open Court, 1986.

—— "Responses." *Inquiry* 37 (1994): 495–505.

—— *The Roots of Reference.* La Salle, Ill.: Open Court, 1973.

—— *Theories and Things.* Cambridge, Mass.: Harvard University Press, 1981.

—— *Word and Object.* Cambridge, Mass.: MIT Press, 1960.

Ramsey, F. P. "Facts and Propositions." In *The Foundations of Mathematics,* pp. 138–155. New York: Humanities Press, 1950.

—— "Truth and Probability." In *Philosophical Papers,* ed. D. H. Mellor. Cambridge: Cambridge University Press, 1990.

—— "Universals." In *Philosophical Papers,* ed. D. H. Mellor. Cambridge: Cambridge University Press, 1990.

Rodenbeck, Max. "Witch Hunt in Egypt." *New York Review of Books,* November 16, 2000, pp. 39–42.

Rorty, Richard. *Consequences of Pragmatism.* Minneapolis: University of Minnesota Press, 1982.

—— "Pragmatism, Davidson, and Truth." In *Truth and Interpretation,* ed. E. Lepore, pp. 333–355. New York: Blackwell, 1986.

—— "Representation, Social Practice, and Truth." *Philosophical Studies* 30 (1988): 215–228.

Russell, Bertrand. *Logic and Knowledge: Essays 1901–1950,* ed. Robert C. Marsh. London: Allen & Unwin, 1956.

—— "On the Nature of Truth and Falsehood." In *Philosophical Essays*, pp. 147–159. New York: Simon and Schuster, 1966.

—— *Principles of Mathematics*. Cambridge: Cambridge University Press, 1903.

—— *The Problems of Philosophy*. Oxford: Oxford University Press, 1959.

Sayre, K. M. *Plato's Late Ontology: A Riddle Resolved*. Princeton: Princeton University Press, 1983.

Schlick, Moritz. "Über das Fundament der Erkenntnis." *Erkenntnis* 4 (1934): 79–99.

Sellars, Wilfrid. *Naturalism and Ontology*. Atascadero, Calif.: Ridgeview, 1981.

—— "Towards a Theory of Predication." In *How Things Are*, ed. J. Bogen and J. E. McGuire, pp. 285–322. Dordrecht: Reidel, 1985.

Soames, Scott. "What Is a Theory of Truth?" *Journal of Philosophy* 81 (1984): 411–429.

Strawson, P. F. "The Asymmetry of Subjects and Predicates." In *Language, Belief, and Metaphysics,* ed. H. E. Kiefer and M. K. Munitz, pp. 96–115. New York: State University of New York Press, 1970. Reprinted in *Logico-Linguistic Papers*.

—— *Logico-Linguistic Papers*. London: Methuen, 1971.

—— "My Philosophy." In *The Philosophy of P. F. Strawson*, ed. P. K. Sen and R. R. Verma, pp. 1–18. New Delhi: Indian Council of Philosophical Research, 1995.

—— "Singular Terms and Predication." *Journal of Philosophy* 58 (1961): 393–412. Reprinted in *Logico-Linguistic Papers*.

—— *Subject and Predicate in Logic and Grammar*. London: Methuen, 1974.

—— "Truth." *Proceedings of the Aristotelian Society,* Supplementary Volume 24 (1950): 129–156. Reprinted in *Logico-Linguistic Papers*.

Tait, W. W., ed. *Early Analytic Philosophy: Frege, Russell, Wittgenstein*. Chicago: Open Court, 1997.

Tarski, Alfred. "The Concept of Truth in Formalized Languages." In *Logic, Semantics, Metamathematics,* ed. J. H. Woodger, pp. 152–278. New York: Oxford University Press, 1956.

—— "The Establishment of Scientific Semantics." In *Logic, Semantics, Metamathematics,* ed. J. H. Woodger, pp. 401–408. New York: Oxford University Press, 1956.

———— "The Semantic Conception of Truth." *Philosophy and Phenomenological Research* 4 (1944): 341–376.

Tugendhat, Ernst. *Vorlesungen zur Einführung in der sprachanalytische Philosophie* [*Traditional and Analytical Philosophy*]. Frankfurt: Suhrkamp, 1976.

van Heijenoort, J. "Logic as Calculus and Logic as Language." *Synthese* 17 (1967): 324–330.

————, ed. *From Frege to Gödel: A Source Book in Mathematical Logic.* Source Books in the History of the Sciences. Cambridge, Mass.: Harvard University Press, 1967.

Vlastos, Gregory. *Socrates.* Cambridge: Cambridge University Press, 1991.

Weiner, Joan. *Frege in Perspective.* Ithaca: Cornell University Press, 1990.

Williams, Michael. "Do We (Epistemologists) Need a Theory of Truth?" *Philosophical Topics* 54 (1986): 223–242.

———— "Epistemological Realism and the Basis of Skepticism." *Mind* 97 (1988): 415–439.

———— "Scepticism and Charity." *Ratio* (New Series), 1 (1988): 176–194.

Wilson, Neil. "Substances without Substrata." *Review of Metaphysics* 12 (1959): 521–539.

Wittgenstein, Ludwig. *Notebooks 1914–1916,* trans. G. E. M. Anscombe. Oxford: Blackwell, 1961.

———— *Tractatus-Logico Philosophicus,* trans. C. K. Ogden. London: Routledge & Kegan Paul, 1922.

Index

Anscombe, Elizabeth, 111–112
Antirealism: of Dummett, 33, 42, 45–47; vs. realism, 33–34, 47–48
Aristotle: on predication, 5, 77, 88–93, 94–95, 96, 117, 147, 156; on Plato's theory of forms, 5, 88–93, 100, 126; on truth, 22, 38, 126–127, 144, 150; and relations, 83, 83n, 104–105; on universals, 89–90, 92, 93–94, 126–127, 143–144, 156; on verbs and names, 90–93, 95, 104, 105, 143–144; *De Interpretatione*, 90–92; *Categories*, 91; on the copula, 91n, 93–94, 95
Assertability, warranted, 45–47
Austin, J. L., 122
Axiomatic theories of truth, 31–32, 31n, 154, 160

Barwise, Jon, 129
Belief, 57–63; relationship to truth, 28, 29, 34, 38–39, 42–43, 43n14, 47, 58–60, 65, 66–67, 68–74, 75, 75n, 120–121; degree of, 58–60, 65–67, 68–73
Bi-conditionals, 25n41, 54
Bivalence, principle of, 45
Black, Max, 15; on Tarski, 148n7, 149

Boyd, Richard, 33
Bradley, F. H., 105–106, 115, 144
Burge, Tyler, 3, 50n

Carnap, Rudolf, 43, 148n7
Charity, principle of, 62–63
Church, Alonzo: on correspondence theories of truth, 6, 40, 40n9, 127–129, 132–133
Coherence theories of truth, 2, 38, 42–43, 43n14, 47
Commands, 53n6, 123, 124, 141, 142
Connectives, truth-functional. *See* Sentential connectives, truth-functional
Convention-T, 20, 23, 26, 28, 30, 31, 34–35, 151–152, 153, 154
Copula, the, 76, 91, 95–96, 103–104, 113, 135, 144, 146, 147; Aristotle on, 91n, 93–94, 95
Cornford, F. M., 83n
Correspondence theories of truth, 2, 124–130; and facts, 6, 39–40, 107, 125–130, 155–156; Frege on, 6, 40, 40n9, 127, 128, 132–133; Church on, 6, 40, 40n9, 127–129, 132–133; Dewey on, 8; and Tarski, 23, 37–38, 41, 155–156; criticisms

173